T0165951

A HEALTHY RIVALRY

Louvain Theological and Pastoral Monographs is a publishing venture whose purpose is to provide those involved in pastoral ministry throughout the world with studies inspired by Louvain's long tradition of theological excellence within the Roman Catholic tradition. The volumes selected for publication in the series are expected to express some of today's finest reflection on current theology and pastoral practice.

LOUVAIN THEOLOGICAL & PASTORAL MONOGRAPHS

—————————————— 20 ——————————————

A HEALTHY RIVALRY

HUMAN RIGHTS IN THE CHURCH

by Rik Torfs

PEETERS PRESS
LOUVAIN

W.B. EERDMANS

This subject has also been treated in Dutch:
Mensen en rechten in de Kerk, Leuven, Davidsfonds, 1993.

Cover: Noah's Ark. Engraving contained in a biblical commentary
published in 1690 by Wilhelmus Goeree, Amsterdam.

ISBN 90-6831-762-8
D. 1995/0602/113

CONTENTS

Foreword   1

I. Human Rights and the Church: A Difficult
   Combination   5
   Historical Ambivalence   5
   A Shift in the Issue, and Terminological
   Misunderstandings   7
   Power, Orthodoxy and the Vision of Law . . .   14
   Balance and Perspectives   18

II. A Dynamic Vision of Law   23
   Law and Theology   23
   Differing Legal Traditions   25
   Open Legal Norms   28
   Canon Law on Three Levels   32
   Juridical Consequences and Theological
   Compromises   36
   Conclusion   38

III. The Genesis and Present Situation of Human
   Rights in the Church   41
   History   41
   The Legal Nature of the Obligations and Rights
   of All Christian Faithful   47

IV. An Overview of the Obligations and Rights of
   All Christian Faithful   55
   Catalogue   55
   The Principle of Equality   56
   Freedom of Expression   59

Freedom of Theological Research 63
Concluding Considerations and Guidelines . . 67

V. Toward a Thorough Culture of Law 69
Rowing Upstream 69
Statute of the Obligations and Rights of All
Christians 73
Protection of Rights 77
The Long Road 82

VI. Fundamental Rights and Independent
Responsibility 87
An Approach that Takes the Initiative 87
The Horizontal Operation of Fundamental
Rights 90
Fundamental Rights and the Common Good . 91
Parallel Circuits 94
Internal Emigration and Schism 99
Personal Responsibility and the Place of the
Hierarchy 100

VII. In Search of Healthy Rivalry 105
Lines of Force and Conclusions 105
The Context of the Present Argument 108
Why not Less Action and More Trust? 110
Why not More Action and Less Trust? 113
In Search of Healthy Rivalry 118

Select Bibliography 121

FOREWORD

The old ideologies seem to be spent. What now? Of course there are still limousines to ride around in and heated swimming pools to float around in, but they lack mystery, the silent strength of unending fascination. They are much too physically present to reflect something of the vulnerable imperishability for which people still yearn in their craziest and in their finest moments. No, actually this is the perfect moment for a revival of Christianity. The message of the gospel has certainly not lost any of its brilliance. Not one single historical fact has brought to light any possible existential weakness in it. The gospel remains at the same time highly demanding yet merciful; it continues to radiate the sublime paradox. But in spite of these encouraging reports Christianity is flickering like a candle in the wind. Research in a number of countries indicates that the issue is not critique of Jesus and his message. Rather, a very great skepticism or indifference, even aversion to the institutional Church can be observed.

In the contemporary imagination that institution appears to be either folkloric or authoritarian — or even worse, an unusual, even bizarre, mixture of both elements.

What do you do about this as a Christian, someone who belongs to a Roman Catholic Church whose vicissitudes you perceive now and then from the dark side? What do you do to prevent the emergence of bitterness, that bitterness which threatens to make the irony a little bit less gentle? Indeed, what do you do about it, for in spite of everything you would prefer nothing more than a Church which radiates vitality and inspiration.

There are a number of ways to help build a more vital Church. The first possibility consists of seeking out what is positive. There is no need to train an eagle eye on the situation to observe that positive elements can be found in many places. Impelled by the gospel, a merciless mirror for half-hearted commitment, many Christians all over the world passionately commit themselves where sorrow prevails or danger threatens, where there is no money to be earned or no glory to be achieved: in the former Yugoslavia, in Africa, but also here in our midst. It would be horrible if tender concern for people who are old, sick, lonely or simply eccentric were only given by pets. Christians are capable of doing a great deal, and in fact they do it. Now and then they fall short in the mission of giving the message of Jesus concrete expression, but we need not create false dilemmas between perfect purity and the death of the last ideal as a result of a heartless puritanism. Even a bit of hypocrisy, while not exactly a precious jewel, is no disaster. It often points to a struggle for something better. Give me a little hesitant hypocrisy any day instead of the so-called authentic barbarity of pure self-interest.

But is this the only way to clean up the tarnished image of the Church? Do we need to focus our gaze exclusively on the many areas where Christians, Church members, create beautiful things out of their inspiration — or at least risk, and continue to risk, making a sublime effort? After all, isn't that far more important than the issue of authority, organization or structure?

Although I would answer the last question in the affirmative without much hesitation, I believe as well that the discussion of Church structures and legal relationships within the Church may not under any circumstances be pushed aside. For those who live attentively, it is not only the more important question that counts, but also the second-most-important, which often displays striking connections with the former. And even though a little hypocrisy is no disaster, the split between Church structures and the gospel has to be kept within liveable limits. I know quite well that there are an infinite number of reasons to keep everything connected with intra-Church issues enveloped in deep silence: the aforementioned relative importance of structures, the fear of aggravating the authorities in Rome which could lead to the nomination of undesirable bishops, the anxiety over making a mistake fatal to one's own career, the danger of alienating even more people from the Church if the Church seems to be a collection of troublemakers, the sorrow of many older people who watch their most beloved certainties break apart. This final argument is the only one I find worthwhile, and it is certainly the most affecting. Still, I believe that the sympathy which hides behind it actually betrays a degree of contempt, or, put more delicately, that the very people one purports to protect are not being taken seriously. Meditation on ecclesial structures with an eye toward their purification, which takes place out of love for the Church, can never cause damage to the believers.

With all this in mind, I believe that writing about human rights in the Church today is a necessity, although one must retain a real sense of modesty. The perfect structures which the Church does not possess at the present moment cannot be found in this book either. While writing I was constantly reminded of the passage by Ivan Klíma in his novel *Love and Rubbish*: "Human beings always continue to long for a return to the place where they have once been in their innocence; but they suspect as well that they shall never again reach it in the time and space allotted to them as human beings, but only in a dimension in which God moves." I believe that this is the case. But that doesn't mean that I do not take seriously, in the depths of my heart, the ideas I set forth here. If there is now and then a bit of irony lurking between the lines, it is not due to iconoclastic sarcasm, but rather due to skepticism concerning my own standpoint or out of hesitation in the face of what is truly precious.

In spite of the fact that those who love absolute truth will not find this book to their liking, I still hope that they at least participate in the discussion, because that is the book's intention. Somewhere between merciless take-no-prisoners battle and cloying flattery, we must urgently make a habitable space for the legitimate difference of opinions which expresses a motto which can hardly be surpassed: *in via veritas.*

CHAPTER I

HUMAN RIGHTS AND THE CHURCH:
A DIFFICULT COMBINATION

Historical Ambivalence

The role which has been played by the Roman Catholic Church in regard to human rights in society can be called, at best, ambivalent.

On the one hand, one cannot escape the conclusion that the Christian ethos, and sometimes the Church itself, has contributed to making the concept of human rights plausible and to its refinement in the Western world. The arrogance of brute force was often corrected by Christianity, however imperfect and not infrequently domineering the latter could be. In 1895 the German jurist Georg Jellinek located the origin of human rights, as they exist today, in the freedom of religion and of conscience which society has sought to enforce on the level of religion since the Reformation.[1] We could question whether this is entirely true: in addition to religion, political power-relations and philosophical ideas play an explicit role. But we cannot minimize the key role played by the Church and Christianity in the origin and the development of human rights.

---

[1] G. Jellinek, "Die Erklärung der Menschen- und Bürgerrechte", reprinted in R. Schnur, *Zur Geschichte der Erklärung der Menschenrechte*, Munich, 1974, 1-77.

Opposed to that is the fact that, in a later period, the Church seemed to be everything except an ally of the same human rights. In the title of the written report following a lecture given by Cardinal Roger Etchegaray in 1989 on Christian culture and human rights, the rather provocative (certainly in Catholic circles) motto, "Du rejet à l'engagement" figured prominently.[2] And this rejection is actually a historical fact which can be little changed by historical writing through rose-colored glasses. In his encyclical *Mirari vos* of 15 August 1832 Pope Gregory XVI called freedom of conscience an absurdity, a form of insanity. And in the *Syllabus of Errors* of Pope Pius IX no great improvement can be seen. With a great flourish of rhetoric which sounds considerably better in lengthy Latin sentences than elsewhere, he condemned a number of modern freedoms.[3]

Slowly the Church's standpoint changed. Perhaps the attitude of Pius XII toward the Nazi regime is not free of all criticism, but what happened at that time has certainly had major after-effects in the Church. A positive evaluation of human rights came into existence through a more accommodating attitude toward the world with its political and social dimensions. The way was cleared by two encyclicals of Pope John XXIII, *Mater et Magistra* (1961) and *Pacem in Terris* (1963), and continued through the Second Vatican Council. Two documents in particular achieved a definitive breakthrough, namely the

[2] R. Etchegaray, "Culture chrétienne et droits de l'homme: du rejet à l'engagement", in Fédération Internationale des Universités Catholiques (ed.), *Culture chrétienne et droits de l'homme*, Brussels/Louvain-la-Neuve, 1991, 3-15.

[3] On this point see R. Aubert, "Religious Liberty from *Mirari Vos* to the *Syllabus*", *Concilium* 1:7 (1965) 89-105.

pastoral constitution *Gaudium et Spes* on the Church in the world in our time, and the declaration *Dignitatis Humanae* on freedom of religion. Equality and other human rights were treated here in a broad perspective. Since then the Church has struggled consistently for human rights in the world. The post-conciliar Popes were all committed supporters of human rights. Human rights are without doubt one of the cornerstones of John Paul II's pontificate. The Church and human rights, formerly enemies, have made peace and are henceforth allies in the struggle.

A Shift in the Issue, and Terminological Misunderstandings

However, the problem was shifted to a different level. While the earlier discussions centered around the theme of human rights *and* the Church, now questions arise concerning human rights *in* the Church. For while the Church authorities denounce general societal abuses, including the abuse of power and the oppression of human persons, the structures of the Church continue to display an authoritarian character. At the head of Part II, Book II, of the Code of Canon Law, issued in 1983, the unequivocal title, "Hierarchical Organization of the Church," still stands.

By referring to this hierarchical structure the Church authorities intend to make clear that the Church (not only its leaders but all its people), does not exercise any domination, and that she herself is subject to divine ordinance. Edward Schillebeeckx observes that on the basis of this argumentation, which to a certain degree is theologically justified, the conclusion is almost magically extracted that democracy is "therefore" not an appropriate model for the Church, which — according to the Flemish theologian — has thus assumed without hesitation the civil forms of royal-authoritarian, feudal and later monarchist forms of government as self-evident.[4]

Is there a place for human rights within such structures? Indeed the contemporary observer can hardly escape the conclusion that Church leaders find it difficult to speak about human rights on their own territory. They will not easily concede that they are anti-, but they are not pro-human rights either. How did that happen? Why don't they roundly applaud the presence of human rights in the Church? Why the long faces, and the long sentences formulated in stammers and peppered with endless nuancing, whenever the subject comes up?

The first problem lies in the concepts (which not infrequently provoke the Church authorities), democracy and human rights.

Democracy: in ecclesiastical circles this concept has a negative connotation, illustrated by the preceding quotation from Edward Schillebeeckx. During discussions one periodically hears someone break into the exchange with the laconic remark, "The Church is not a democracy." Then a deep silence follows and the speaker looks straight ahead, as if a mysterious truth lies hidden behind this short statement, a truth difficult to explain to someone who does not already sense it in some way. The discussion is finished, the lips are pursed shut. But the statement still raises questions. If the Church is not a democracy, how *can* it be characterized? For example,

---

[4] E. Schillebeeckx, *Church: The Human Story of God*, London, 1990, 235.

can we say that the Church is a royal-authoritarian system? Or perhaps, that the Church is an absolute monarchy? Expressions of this sort are rarely made, or at least kept behind closed doors.

But then what *is* the hidden meaning of this short sentence? Is the intention simply to say that the Church, given its own nature, cannot coincide with the form of any state? However, beside the expression "the Church is not a democracy" stands the conclusion that it is not an absolute monarchy either. In fact I have no difficulty with this expression. Ultimately the Church is not so much one political system or another. As both an instrument and a sign of salvation it cannot be fully identified with such systems, and under no circumstances can it fully fall under such a system.

But we should not be naive. The expression "the Church is not a democracy" does not in the first place imply that the Church cannot be identified with any single form of political government. It means primarily that the true nature of the Church cannot be reconciled with a democratic form of government. We come back to the quotation from Schillebeeckx: the Church is not the possessor of God's call, thus there is no room for democracy in the Church. The dilemma is not convincing, and could just as easily be set up between the Church and other forms of government. Government in the Church must always be carried out with God's call in mind, but it must take place. Why not try to find the least oppressive form of government? In this regard democracy should not be seen as an awkward caricature, a view which very often implicitly underlies the thought of those who promote the pseudo-meaningful expression, "the Church is not a democracy." Ultimately democracy may not imply that a tiny majority of 51%, triumphant after a bitter struggle, will mercilessly subject to its will the sizeable minority of 49% under the motto, "The winner takes all," and tough luck to the losers. Modern democracy has nothing to do with the brutal force of the majority. Such a vision is nothing more than a distorted image developed by those who consider the exercise of authority to be necessarily bound up with dictatorship — if not that of the monarch, then that of bare statistics.

Democracy sets more stock by a form of government in which no actual qualitative difference exists between the leaders and the governed. This is expressed in political structures in which the will of the people, expressed from time to time in different majorities, really does play a role. But democracy equally means the existence of appropriate structures for joint management, the organization of adequate legal protection, and genuine concern for each person via fundamental rights, among other things. A government which is transparent and limited, which can justify itself upon request, is also characteristic of democracy in a broad sense.[5] In the view we have just outlined, democracy has little to do with the domination of the minority by the majority, but instead with mechanisms which protect both the individual and the general welfare against lapses by those who hold power. These lapses are intrinsically linked to power itself. If power is no longer held accountable for its actions, it is in danger of showing signs of authoritarianism. The Church's unique nature changes nothing of this deeply human reality.

---

[5] N. Greinacher in E. Drewermann, N. Greinacher and D. Sölle, *Wege der Befreiung sehen*, Ilsede, 1992, 74.

Along with the concept of democracy, the term "human rights" also has a number of meanings. What Paul Valéry said of freedom also applies to human rights: "one of those words which does not so much speak as sing" ("un de ces mots qui chantent plus qu'ils ne parlent"). The elusive aspect of the idea often serves as an excuse to discount it, at least for use within the Church. How dare one speak about human rights in the Church (it is sometimes said), in a world of starvation and war? Human rights have to do with torture, barbed wire, blood on the stake. It's so exaggerated, so petty, in fact so unjust to try to use the term human rights for conflicts in the Church which one (at least in terms of civil law) can leave whenever one pleases. Is it not so that many people sharply protest violations of human rights only when they feel themselves disadvantaged? Human rights function in this way as the last resort for a bad loser; they become a weapon used by a spoiled child. I can't have an ice-cream cone today? A violation of human rights!

A refinement in the term "human rights" is necessary. Whenever the term is employed in discussions within the Church without a precise definition, it generally refers to the Universal Declaration on Human Rights of the United Nations (1948) or to the European Convention on Human Rights as elaborated by the Council of Europe (1950). Those are two very concrete documents which contain well-defined rights and freedoms. The latter text, for that matter, lays out distinct boundaries which are inextricably linked with the law: it is certainly not the individualistic charter of the Me-generation for which enthusiastic supporters of the communal ideal once mistook it. The European Convention, which is applied directly by many countries to their own system of law, displays above all a strong practical importance. It contains in addition to the right to life (art. 2), and the prohibition of torture (art. 3) and slavery (art. 4), directives which certainly arose from tragic and gruesome circumstances, plus other rules which perhaps have less to do with life and death, freedom and servitude, but whose observance is indispensable in a democratic society governed by law. I am thinking for example of the right to an appropriate trial (art. 6), the right to respect for private and family life (art. 8), freedom of thought, conscience and religion (art. 9), freedom of opinion (art. 10). The European Commission and the European Court of Human Rights insure that even these rights will be safeguarded in our European democracies. In addition one can imagine an expansion towards basic social rights within the concept of human rights, but the flexibility of these rights must not be stretched to the breaking point.

There is not a violation of human rights lurking behind every conflict. It is inevitable that, if at least two candidates have applied for the same position, one of them will not get it. And the fact that a recommendation might not be followed always and everywhere has to do with the difference between a consultative and a legislative prerogative. The uncomfortable feeling aroused by a sharp difference of opinion is not necessarily connected to a violation of human rights.

I think that the terms democracy and human rights are not infrequently perceived, consciously or unconsciously, as caricatures by church leaders and by persons who are suspicious of greater openness in the Church. In this sense what I have said up to now is not a refutation of ideas that nobody is really expressing, to the greater glory and honor of one's own point of view. It is a well-known rhetorical trick, to set up a "straw man" against whose unnuanced ideas one can easily score points. No, I am sure that a genuine discussion of human rights in the Church would be clouded over from the beginning by misunderstandings about the concepts of democracy and human rights.

If democracy primarily concerns attention to the human person in a constitutional state, then doesn't the idea fit comfortably with the notion of the People of God as outlined in the second chapter of the dogmatic constitution on the Church, *Lumen Gentium*? And if human rights are broader than the right to life, but on the other hand are clearly defined even though violations are possible from time to time on fairly technical grounds, is that not reassuring for the hierarchy of the Church? Certain violations of human rights do not always put at risk the credibility of the entire system of law. Thus my native Belgium has been ruled against several times in the European Court of Human Rights, but no one would deny that Belgium remains a nation in which the rule of law prevails.

But even though a clearer description of basic concepts such as democracy and human rights could clarify and expedite the discussion, it might still be difficult to maintain that the only thing blocking a general acceptance of human rights in the Church up to now is a terminological misunderstanding. There is more going on here. What deeper motives lie behind the great reluctance of the Church's leaders with respect to the issue of human rights in the Church? I see three arguments, which concern respectively power, orthodoxy, and a vision of law.

Power, Orthodoxy and the Vision of Law

The primary argument which comes to mind which could explain the cool reception accorded by the hierarchy to human rights in the Church is the mentality of power. Human rights limit the power of the hierarchy. The authorities suddenly find they have an opponent who can no longer easily be manipulated. And the principle of scarcity is inexorable: if someone can make an appeal to a right, then that immediately reduces the freedom of whoever exercises power over him or her. But I do not really want to go into the question of the mentality of power as an enemy of human rights here. This almost inevitably presupposes bad faith, or the disappearance of authentic inspiration, and I am convinced that this is generally not the case. For the most part, I am willing to assume that the church authorities have the best of intentions.

In its direct form the power mentality of the authorities is in all probability less strongly present than progressive critics of the system would lead us to suspect. In fact it is difficult for anyone to concede power. And, in the same way, it cannot be denied that a major undertaking is involved in leaving behind familiar structures, well-trod paths. The comfort of the familiar is very attractive. Change demands energy. In a system such as the Church in which, at present, conformity is valued more highly than innovation, a potential reformer would have to be strongly motivated to triumph over the natural conservatism that characterizes everyone to some degree. Or, to put it another way, who is going to slave away like mad just to be reproached, as long as well-intentioned laziness leads to high praise?

A second argument against human rights in the Church, or at least against human rights in practice, could be far more substantial. This is the fear on the part of the authorities that making room for human rights in the Church puts orthodoxy at risk. The question is very much whether this fear, which severely cripples the process at times, has any foundation. Does a difference in emotional, esthetic, juridical, political or philosophical positions always also concern orthodoxy? Or is orthodoxy often a concept that conceals differences of opinion which are more esthetic or philosophical in origin? Are we afraid that, for example, changes in organizational structures will erode the core of our faith? Does this not reflect a lack of trust in Jesus and his unsurpassed message?

In his book *Philosophy and the Mirror of Nature*, published in 1979, the American philosopher Richard Rorty distinguishes two approaches to the role of the philosopher.[6]

The first approach regards the philosopher as well-informed dilettante, who endeavors to forge a pragmatic link between differing discourses. Differences of opinion between intellectual disciplines and modes of expression are settled by a compromise or transcended in the course of the conversation, talk or discussion. The method is hermeneutical. This is the style of Socrates.

The second approach regards the philosopher as one possessed of a broader view, as the thinker who takes account of the social basis of the community. He or she knows what everyone else is actually doing, even when they do not quite know themselves. This person always

[6] R. Rorty, *Philosophy and the Mirror of Nature*, Princeton, 1980, 315-356.

knows the ultimate context within which every action takes place. This method is epistemological. This is the style of Plato.

My question is as follows: can Plato, but not Socrates, be reconciled with Christian orthodoxy?

Does this orthodoxy remain convincing only (and I am deliberately caricaturing this), when the believer, even before he or she begins to believe, first assumes the philosophical approach of Plato?

A third reason why human rights in the Church continue to come up against suspicion and hostility, is the vision of law — or its absence — operative among the Church hierarchy. To put it briefly, it comes down to the fact that the ecclesiastical hierarchy is not completely convinced that law has a vital role to play. Law is allotted a functional, technical role. I remember, at a congress of canon lawyers some years ago, the comparison made by a representative of the hierarchy : "For me, the body of the Church (always haltingly) evokes the following image: theology is the brains, spirituality is the heart, pastoral work is the face (which listens, speaks, sees, smells, tastes ... and is seen, heard and felt) and law is the skeleton."[7] It is a prosaic undertaking to build up a life around this skeleton, and continually to meditate upon it and to remain actively engaged with it.

It is no wonder that such a vision of law is coupled with a tendency to reduce the latitude of law as far as possible. For many of those in authority law seems to be too bony, too forbidding, and not pastoral enough. With its uncompromising straightforwardness law drives out love, apparently. Law and love are set in opposition to

---

[7] See R. Torfs, P. De Roo and H. Warnink, eds., *De katholieke iden-titeit van instellingen en organisaties in het recht*, Leuven, 1990, 13.

each other. On the one hand, there is the juridical church, strongly influenced by sociology, a church of trouble-makers, of aggressive people who demand their rights, and calculating customers who file lawsuits. On the other hand, there is the warm church of love, based on Christian community. This church is more than a purely juridi-cally-ordered community, as church leaders are quick to add. They say the church is more than that, but at the same time they often mean it is less. In a church of love, to demand one's rights seems to be a contradiction in terms, an attack on the purity of love.

This dilemma, often implicitly acknowledged, between the church of law and the church of love, must be unmasked. Of course, the canon lawyer cannot act in the way a civil lawyer would. Whoever practices canon law is never allowed to forget that she or he is involved with law in the Church. But, on the other hand, it is also true that law, if it is functional, must be able to operate in an atmosphere of conflict. Conflicts in the Church cannot be resolved through a) the simple announcement that, theo-logically speaking, they cannot exist, or b) the claim that if they do occur, everything must be done so that conflict is not dealt with as conflict, even if the consequence is that the conflict continues or increases in scope.

Let us remain sober, and recognize and love humanity with all its human flaws, even in the Church. Love and law go hand in hand. As long as there is love, law remains in the background where no one can abuse it. But if love slackens, evaporates or disappears for a little while, then there is the lucidity of law, the art of the good and the just. Law is a safety net, a companion to get us through fearful days. Perhaps in itself it offers fewer pos-sibilities than a pastoral approach, but it certainly offers more than a pseudo-pastoral one, and these two items seem to lie frightfully close to each other whenever love loses something of its power. Or to put it another way, good law is certainly more pastoral than a dubious pastoral approach. And this is more than a slogan. Just knowing that one can depend on law gives a fantastically good feeling, a feeling which many people on this earth can scarcely dream of. No more than law (unfortunately, perhaps!) but certainly no less (fortunately).

It is clear that the approach we have outlined, with love and law as complementary concepts, presumes a vision of law which greatly diverges from the minimalist notion of a "skeleton." For me law is not an unchangeable package of norms. On the contrary, it leaves space for interpretation which is always a bit uncertain, for options regarding content, for points of view, for the intellect, the heart, and the face — in short, for the whole person.

Balance and Perspectives

The title of this chapter points to the tension between human rights and Church, a tension which is not yet resolved.

With respect to the refinement of human rights in society, the role of the Church is ambivalent. On the one hand, it acted as a stimulant while, on the other hand, it showed itself to be a strong opponent of modern freedoms, especially in the nineteenth century. The tide turns very late, and very slowly. Today the Church speaks out enthusiastically and without restraint in favor of human rights in our secular society.

Now that the fight is joined, a new front has opened up — that of human rights in the Church. God's call is invoked in order to undercut democratic structures. Even human rights run into a great deal of mistrust and opposition on the part of ecclesial dignitaries.

Part of this negative attitude can be attributed to vague terminology. A refinement of the concepts of democracy and human rights could bring some relief on this point.

But Church leaders are driven into a defensive position by even deeper motives. I can give three of these. The mentality of power is one of them, although it is less directly involved than one might suspect. Perhaps more important is a thought that is related to it — the present-day climate in the Church rewards caution and striving to maintain the status-quo. A second factor is the fear on the part of Church authorities that human rights threaten orthodoxy. And finally, a miserly view of law — law as the "skeleton" — certainly does not invite enthusiastic arguments in favor of human rights in the Church. How can we move further, starting from this basis, in the direction of a more positive appreciation of human rights in the Church? There are two paths I prefer not to take, that of history and that of science-fiction. In both cases the temptation is strong.

History always offers good points of departure for depicting pure forms of faith-communities and passing them along as models. One feels a sort of homesickness, above all regarding the first Christians. When we appeal to them as an authority, it often seems that to the degree that time passes — and more historical sources become known? — a steadily increasing deterioration overtakes both Church and Christianity. In itself this is not a very attractive thought. In any case, I do not subscribe to it. The fact that models from the past must be seen in their own context and cannot simply be applied here and there from out of the mists of time certainly needs no further comment.

There is also the temptation to launch into science-fiction, a discipline against which I actually have certain esthetic reservations before the discussion even begins. Particularly theologians who are in the habit of claiming that current canon law is not exactly smoothly connected with the theology of the Second Vatican Council (conveniently forgetting the ambivalence within the Council itself) hold that structural changes are inevitable. Regularly they formulate concrete suggestions as well. Whenever their suggestions are irreconcilable with the 1983 Code of Canon Law, however, they are simply a voice in the wilderness. The same story is told over and over again, for years. The arguments against mandatory celibacy for priests or against the ordination of women to the priesthood, for example, have remained absolutely the same for decades. This stagnation drives people to dispair and puts young people off. In which branch of art or science can we find exactly the same discussion, with the same arguments down to the smallest details, carried out today as ten years ago? The irony is that precisely in connection with these types of problems, problems which have already been thoroughly analyzed in theological literature, such as mandatory celibacy for clergy or the ordination of women, church leaders not infrequently insist on the necessity of further study because the file is not yet complete. Agoraphobia is sublimated into an insatiable appetite for in-depth study and reflection. By this I am not trying to drive every form of utopian thought into the ground. It would be unacceptable for a Christian to shrink from dreaming and struggling for ideal structures, and to be thrown back exclusively on *Realpolitik*. But to aim for nothing other than distant dreams, without developing alternatives that would help to make life today somewhat more bearable, does not seem to me to be the best way.

Neither ruminations about the past nor futuristic constructions are satisfying when they are the only answer to the contemporary issues within the Church, although one can manage to understand both approaches in the joyless atmosphere of retrenchment which is suffocatingly present here and there in the contemporary Church.

At the same time I believe that there are also possibilities for hope which are born out of, and are in agreement with, the present church structures. There is a possible strategy for resistance and submission within the church, which might indeed question the existing structures but at the same time accepts them as its point of departure. This strategy colors the story to follow. The reader will search the following pages in vain for what one might call an "objective analysis of human rights in the Church," for the simple reason that it does not exist ...

In the chapters to follow I will undertake an attempt to sketch possibilities for renewal in the Church and for genuine warmth in the life of a modern community of faith, starting from existing canon law, in which I see an important role for human rights. The method chosen for this task is cumulative in nature.

In the second chapter I will try to clarify the possibilities for law in the Church. The fact that I was not particularly pleased with the image of law as a skeleton is already clear. How can light be shed on law whereby law would not only become more powerful in content, but in addition can contribute to building a Church which liberates itself from oppressive structures?

After developing an idea of law which has more flexibility and liberating power than is usual today, we can
look in the canon law code currently in force to find concrete norms of law which are linked with human rights
and to which the juridical vision of Chapter Two can be
applied.

Only thereafter, that is, after a clear vision of law has
been outlined and a careful inventory taken of the legal
guidelines to which this vision can be applied, can we
begin to work on a concrete strategy which, entirely
legally, can make a contribution, on the basis of human
rights, to a practical renewal of the Church which leads to
more joy and openness.

CHAPTER II

A DYNAMIC VISION OF LAW

Law and Theology

Discussions concerning law which take place within my professional field, canon law, tend to deal with other things. They limit themselves to thought experiments on the relationship between law and theology. At first sight this type of approach may be surprising. After all, reflections on the essence and function of civil law are not confined to the relationship between law and ethics, or possible links between law and philosophy.

The enthusiasm with which canon lawyers throw themselves into the relation between law and theology can be explained historically. The previous Code of Canon Law of 1917 is generally interpreted in a positivist way. The law stood for itself. Generally no questions were asked about the motivations of the legislator or which theological ideas lay at its roots. *Dura lex, sed lex* (a severe law, but a law). The result of this attitude was that canon law was not exactly a well-loved discipline, and almost no one showed much spontaneous interest in it. A few seminarians who would have preferred to study exegesis or astronomy were sent off against their will to take on canon law. Colleagues waved goodbye with expressions of sympathy.

The turnabout came at the time of the Second Vatican Council. Thereafter laws were required to have a solid theological basis. The present Code of Canon Law (1983) was built on the same principle. In the apostolic constitution *Sacrae disciplinae leges*, Pope John Paul II wrote that, in a certain way, the new Code should be seen as a tremendous effort to express the doctrine of the Second Vatican Council, and especially its ecclesiology, in the language of canon law.[8]

Discussion in the field of the theory of law also focuses on the question of the relationship between canon law and theology. The school of Navarra defends the position that law and theology must be clearly distinguished, in spite of the external connection between the two. The administration and magisterium of the Church always exercise control over canon law. The Munich school, on the other hand, holds that no essential distinction can be made any longer between canon law and theology. They are both theological disciplines and differ solely in method.[9]

For outsiders the whole discussion might appear eccentric. It is theoretical in nature and does not always seem to take account of the possibility that law, apart from its relationship to theology, might have its own story to tell. In fact the specific dynamism of law is constantly overlooked. This climate, in which all the attention is focused on the theological orientation of canon law, explains a number of very rudimentary and static views on law, such as the notion of law as a skeleton. But there are moments when even the outspokenly theologically-oriented canonist cannot escape the deeper issues related to law.

[8] Apostolic Constitution *Sacrae Disciplinae Leges, Acta Apostolicae Sedis*, 25 January 1983, vol. 75, part II, p. vii.

[9] For further details and for a description of other schools, see M. Wijlens, *Theology and Canon Law: The Theories of Klaus Mörsdorf and Eugenio Corecco*, Lanham/New York/London, 1992, 11-22.

Differing Legal Traditions

Present-day canon law, which can be found for the most part in the 1983 Code, is primarily influenced by Roman law and the continental legal tradition. This is not a scandal, of course, although one could imagine that a legal system which is valid for the universal Church might let itself be inspired by other legal traditions as well.

Now and then, for example at an international congress, a culture shock occurs which suddenly sheds light on the implicit presuppositions underlying the ecclesial system of law. Why should canon law depend for support on legal texts, as is the case in the continental traditions? Would it not be equally possible, following the lines of Anglo-American legal procedure, to pay attention to judicial rulings and the legal precedents they create? Wouldn't a more analytical approach offer a number of possibilities, such as a sharper focus on concrete cases, which would tend to remain in the shadows in a more synthetic continental approach?

In a paper presented in 1980 at a congress on fundamental rights in the Church, the Canadian canonist Germain Lesage proposed a more inductive methodology, which he illustrated with an uncommonly fine comparison by the late British prime minister Harold MacMillan: "Latin minds begin by intellectual planning. They give shape to the landscape by roads and towns, aquaducts and villas. The model they create is transferred from paper onto the soil. Non-latin minds create their projects by allowing them to develop slowly according to the natural features of the land. Thus an irregular mosaic is created in full harmony with hills, vegetation and water-ways."[10]

This quotation aptly illustrates my point. The Anglo-American *common law* system, by preferring the precedent as the basis for its judgements, develops from case to case. The rule of law is not so much the product of a universal juridical principle, as it is the generalization of a concrete solution. In each case the judge looks for the *ratio decidendi*, the binding rule of law from earlier cases, in order to reach a solution. The rule of law, although of a general nature which exceeds the particular case, remains closely connected with the concrete circumstances from which it developed. Both judges and lawyers argue inductively.[11] The Western continental tradition works quite differently, that is, in a deductive way using abstract principles. The rule of law has often been drawn up in abstract terms by the legislator in order to comprise all possible future cases. So this procedure is just the reverse, as illustrated perfectly by the MacMillan quote.

The preceding text makes it clear that the question of how to deal with law in the Church has not been adequately answered simply because that law has attained a place in theological thinking. Various juridical approaches are possible. There are more than just the continental and the Anglo-American approaches, of course; for example, there is the *palaver*, the conciliatory model of continual

---

[10] G. Lesage, "Les droits fondamentaux de la personne dans le perspective du 'Common Law'", in E. Corecco, N. Herzog and A. Scola, eds., *Les droits fondamentaux du chrétien dans l'église et dans la société*, Fribourg/Freiburg im B./Milan, 1981, 848.

[11] See F. Gorlé, G. Bourgeois and H. Bocken, *Rechtsvergelijking*, Ghent, 1985, 177; M.A. Glendon, M.W. Gordon and C. Osakwe, *Comparative Legal Traditions*, St. Paul (MN), 1985.

dialogue, which comes from the Bantu legal tradition. Theologically speaking, it would be hard to say that one or another idea of law is superior or inferior. The Anglo-American legal tradition is not more distant from God than the continental, nor is there any radical option in the Gospel for the Western continental system of law. Yet it is hard to escape the impression that the continental approach suits an institution such as the Church. Laws which are perfectly clear seem to offer more stability than an elusive, fuzzy form of jurisprudence; and a legal system built on "palavers" would be more closely related to a dialogical model of church than to the hierarchical model as we know it today.

Should we conclude from all this that canon law, as heir to the continental tradition, constitutes a fixed normative entity which must not be tampered with? Is this still the notion of canon law as a skeleton? I do not think so.

For one thing, the Church's preference for the continental model is only an implicit one. It should not by any means be taken as the only frame of reference. For example, in the field of marriage law, the rulings of the Roman Rota play a guiding role which shows links with the Anglo-American tradition. In fact, canon law practice is most developed in the field of marriage law, resulting in a variety of thorough legal discussions.

Secondly, the existence of a specific law does not necessarily imply that that law is unequivocal. It does not state what it states. This principle does not only hold true for poetry. The fact that a rule of law constitutes a norm does not exempt it from the principle that it is only communicable through language. I would like to dwell for a moment upon one concrete aspect typical of the wording of such norms.

Open Legal Norms

The canons in the Code of Canon Law contain quite a few open norms of law. Concepts such as "scandal," "common good," "just punishment," "respect," or "obedience" can hardly be designated by any other name. Where does this flood of open, multivalent legal norms come from? There are two decisive factors.

To begin, we cannot escape the fact that canon law has to do with the juridical organization of a community of faith. This implies that themes other than bank statements and tax returns are of primary interest. Faith demands a different, less univocal language. The effect of this fact can also be observed in canon law. However, to be satisfied with the idea that the unique character of the Church entails the use of a distinctive vocabulary reveals a certain smugness characteristic of *sui generis* reasoning which shuns every comparison.

There could be a second reason for the massive presence of vague legal norms in canon law, namely, the absence of a system for the separation of powers within the Church. To be sure, Canon 135, par. 1 in the Code of Canon Law states that governmental power is divided into legislative, executive and judicial powers. But the significance of this paragraph is very limited; the governmental powers are *distinguished*, but not *separated*. There is a technical distinction among them, but in fact they are all exercised by one central figure: the bishop in his diocese, and the Pope in the universal Church.

Of course I am aware that the separation of powers is not an unequivocal concept. There is a difference between Locke who gives prominence to the legislator, and Montesquieu who, via a sociological analysis of the underlying social forces at work, develops a legal theory of the state concerning the functions which must be fulfilled to permit society to realize its *esprit*, its own spirit.[12] Moreover, the idea of the separation of three independent powers has been superseded. Already in 1921 the Dutch specialist in constitutional law, C.W. van der Pot, declared that the system had long become obsolete, and one reason was the increasing blurring of legislative and executive tasks within the European parliamentary democracies.[13]

What certainly continues to characterize the separation of powers is the idea of balance and control, for which an impartial and independent judiciary is of particularly great value. That is precisely what is missing in the Church: there is no independent judge who will pore over legal texts to resolve a concrete dispute. This leaves the legislator free to avoid issuing perfectly clear and sharply outlined legal provisions, in the interest of keeping the body of ideas intact and implementing them in society. Why should the legislator bother to compose technically flawless laws, if he is the same one who will later interpret their range and application in his capacity as supreme judge? The judicial power is not independent, there is no external control, so why bother? At the same time, since there is no separation of powers, the legislator not only does not suffer any disadvantage as a result of vague laws, but even benefits by them. The legislator wields executive power as well, so that the more open a particular law is, the more room for policy-making as an executive. Tight rules would only prove a hindrance in devising policy.

---

[12] On this topic see J. Witteveen, *Evenwicht van machten*, Zwolle, 1991, 50-51.

[13] C.W. van der Pot, *De verdeling der Staatstaak*, Haarlem, 1921, 8.

It appears from what has been said up to now that the presence of a great number of open legal norms in canon law can be attributed to two causes. One is that the specific character of law for a community of faith leads toward open laws. And, further, the absence of a separation of powers in the Church excuses the legislator from making sharply defined laws. On the contrary, in his capacity as executive the legislator has a vested interest in maintaining a shroud of vagueness around laws.

Does all of this imply that the whole system, with its vague laws, is simply an instrument in the hands of a hierarchical authority which holds all power in a single hand? That conclusion would be false. The existence of numerous open legal norms can be explained in part by the concentration of power in the Church, but their presence can be put to good use by others besides the hierarchy. Open legal norms are open for everyone, and even ordinary lay people can profit by them. Laws exist in themselves, for whatever reason they might be as they are. The text of the law is primary.

This same idea can be found in Canon 17 of the Code of Canon Law, which gives guidelines for interpreting the text of a law: "Ecclesiastical laws are to be understood in accord with the proper meaning of the words considered in their text and context. If the meaning remains doubtful and obscure, recourse is to be taken to parallel passages, if such exist, to the purpose and the circumstances of the law, and to the mind of the legislator."[14]

---

[14] See R. Torfs, "*Propria verborum significatio*: de l'épistémologie à l'herméneutique", *Studia Canonica* 29 (1995) 179-192.

So the intention of the legislator comes at the end of a line which begins with the meaning of the words as such. The meaning of Canon 17 can be agreed upon, irrespective of whether its proper meaning exists at all, or whether every recognized meaning does not at least imply a value judgment. The will of the legislator must not take precedence. The legislator is expected to know how to express his intentions verbally. This is not a new idea. Such a highly authoritative author as Francisco Suárez (1548-1617) wrote that a law does not originate through the will of the legislator, but through the words of the law.[15] That is what is so attractive about the law. Whatever may be the intentions which gave rise to the Code of Canon Law, and however undemocratically decisions were reached, at a certain moment, on 25 January 1983, it was promulgated: ten months later, on the first Sunday of Advent, it became law. From that moment on a Code has a life of its own. This is too often forgotten. As mentioned before, the monopoly enjoyed by the hierarchy in creating the law is often implicitly and unjustly still assumed to be operative at the level of its interpretation.

Although the Code of Canon Law is issued by the Pope — the well-known Dutch canonist Ruud Huysmans in his numerous publications consistently calls it "the Papal Code"[16] — it can of course be read on very different levels. Open legal norms contribute to expanding the possibilities for such a reading.

---

[15] F. Suárez, *Tractatus de legibus ac Deo legislatore*, Antwerp, 1613, i, VI, C.1, no. 13.
[16] See, for example, R.G.W. Huysmans, *Het recht van de leek in de rooms-katholieke kerk van Nederland*, Hilversum, 1986.

Canon Law on Three Levels

Roughly speaking, the Code of Canon Law can be approached from three levels: macro-, meso- and micro-level.

The macro-level consists of assuming the position of the Pope and his staff. From this vantage point it is clear that the Holy Father retains considerable scope for policy-making. His is the highest, most complete, immediate and universal power within the Church, power which he can freely wield at all times (Canon 331). The list of powers, which sounds somewhat pompous to our modern ears, is more than just a piece of rhetoric. Canon 331 par. 1 grants the Pope legal precedence in ordinary power over all the particular churches and groups. This means that he not only holds power over the church as a whole, but that he can personally, directly — and decisively — interfere anywhere in the world. Canon 333, par. 3 suppresses any glimmer of doubt about this by stating that there is no appeal or recourse against any papal statement or decree. Reading the Code from this angle, at the macro-level, makes one feel that whoever happens *not* to be Pope, and there are quite a few of those in the Church, will be left with no more than a few crumbs.

It is also possible, however, to look at the Code from a meso perspective, that is to say, from the bishop's position. What can he do within the structure of the present Code, if he wants to make more room for liberating structures? He certainly holds far more trump cards than most bishops themselves seem to realize.

First, the bishop functions as the interpreter of the universal law. Precisely because a great many legal norms are somewhat vague, they conceal quite a few possibilities. Just one example: in Canon 861, par. 2 it says that if the ordinary minister, namely the bishop, priest or deacon is impeded, the local ordinary can nominate others to administer baptism validly. Now the question is, what should be understood by the word "impeded?" Here the discussion remains open. Does it mean that no cleric can be found within a range of fifty kilometers? Or that clerics who might be available must be on holiday, or ill? Or could it mean that, for the sake of efficient pastoral care, clerics must not be overburdened with duties which can be performed just as well by a pastoral worker? Legally this last interpretation is perfectly acceptable.

But the bishop has a few more cards to play, so to speak. He may promulgate particular laws within his own diocese, although the possibilities are not limitless. Canon 135, par. 2 *in fine* states in no uncertain terms that a lower legislator cannot issue a law which is contrary to a law enacted by a higher authority. Again, this does not mean that in such a case the bishop is powerless against universal law. In his executive capacity he still has quite a few possibilities open to him. The 1983 Code vastly broadens the bishop's authority to provide dispensations from universal law.[17] While according to Canon 81 in the 1917 Code of Canon Law, the bishop could not in principle dispense from universal laws, the present Canon 87, par. 1 states the exact opposite: "As often as he judges that a dispensation will contribute to the spiritual good of the faithful, the diocesan bishop can dispense from both universal and particularly disciplinary laws established for

---

[17] On this topic see R.G.W. Huysmans, "The Significance of Particular Law and the Nature of Dispensation as Questions on the Rule of Papal Law", in J. Provost and K. Walf, eds., *Ius sequitur vitam: Studies in Canon Law Presented to P.J.M. Huizing*, Leuven, 1991, 44-45.

this territory or for his subjects by the supreme authority of the church. He cannot dispense, however, from procedural or penal laws or from those laws whose dispensation is especially reserved to the Apostolic See or to another authority."

Certainly there are still more limitations to the bishop's power of dispensation, apart from what is stated here. Canon 85 states that dispensations are only possible regarding purely ecclesiastical laws; and Canon 86 exempts from dispensation all laws containing essential constituent elements of juridical institutes or acts. Moreover, no dispensation is allowed without a just and reasonable cause (Canon 90). But even if dispensation should be impossible, the bishop is not helpless. He can resort to a "go-slow" action. Without actually rejecting the law itself, the bishop can reduce its application. With regard to certain of his duties as a member of the executive power, he can adopt a kind of sluggishness. For instance, in order to prevent the function of permanent deacons in the liturgy from issuing in a situation which is detrimental to women, he could proclaim a moratorium on the ordination of deacons, something already practiced by the former bishop of Seattle, R. Hunthausen, and by bishop F. Sullivan of Richmond. Although this practice is still open to discussion,[18] there is no doubt that, at the meso-level, within a bishop's powers, there are quite a few creative possibilities. To put it briefly, we can speak of a strategy in four stages: the interpretation of the universal law, particular laws, dispensation and go-slow action — not a bad package at all. But the suc-

---

[18] Some canonists argue, not incorrectly, that this moratorium is incompatible with Canon 1026 which strictly forbids deterring a candidate who is canonically suitable from receiving ordination.

cess of its application depends entirely on the figure of the bishop.

In addition to the approach to law from the macro-level (the Pope) and the meso-level (the bishop), the same Code can be read on the micro-level, that is, from the standpoint of the individual Christian. The corner-stone of such an interpretation of the law is the obliga-tions and rights of all the Christian faithful (Canons 208-223). I am convinced that these sixteen canons (some of which are relevant only within the Church and have no connection to basic civil legal rights) contain everything necessary to serve as the liberating launch-pad, as it were, for positive renewal in the Church. If it were the legislator's intention to achieve a structural status quo, it was a mistake to include Canons 208-223 in the Code. For all their vagueness they are a Pandora's box, cer-tainly from a conservative ecclesiastical point of view. We cannot be sure what will result from these provi-sions. They include a number of propositions which might turn out to be explosive. As soon as the principle of equality becomes juridically relevant, it is no longer merely an ornament (Canon 208). How far does the right of association extend (Canon 215)? And what about the right and the duty to express one's views (Canon 212, par. 3)? In the following chapter we will analyze these canons and their scope.

Meanwhile it should be clear that the law in general, and the Code of Canon Law in particular, can be approached from different angles, partly due to the numerous open legal norms which can be found in them. The results of legal investigative processes will vary depending upon the approach taken (macro/meso/micro) without one result being juridically more correct than another. The point of departure may decide the outcome of the legal argument but not its correctness.

Juridical Consequences and Theological Compromises

So far in this chapter an effort has been made to develop a dynamic view of law. The fact that canonical theory of law deals almost exclusively with the theological statute of canon law and almost completely ignores the specific dynamics of law, does not mean that the latter do not exist. The implicit choice of a form of canon law typical of the continental legal tradition is less innocent than it looks: it is an option which guarantees the authorities the highest degree of control. But even within a primarily continental type of legal system a good deal of room for creativity remains because of, among other things, the open legal norms which are especially well-represented in the Code of Canon Law. A dynamic view of law also means that the Code, although conceived in an 'undemocratic' manner, is not bound to that process in its interpretation. On the contrary, the Code can be approached on three different levels, the last of which is that of the individual member of the Church, based on the obligations and rights of all Christian believers as set forth in the Code.

Critics might react by saying that this method of reading the Code on different levels certainly looks interesting but, at the same time, risks causing a sort of short-circuit within the Code itself. Can one, without risk, consider all the juridical consequences of the rights and duties of all Christians without somehow impairing the highest, most complete, immediate and universal ordinary power in the Church, the power of the Pope? I am afraid that we cannot get around the principle of economic scarcity here. More rights for the faithful means less power for the hierarchy, even if there is the fullest possible harmony between the two.

These short-circuits (which are not a figment of the imagination), and the clashes and conflicts which could arise, cannot automatically be blamed on an approach to law from particular standpoints, or on the law in general. They are the result of the theological compromises which can be found in the documents of the Second Vatican Council. For instance, in the constitution on the Church the doctrine of papal primacy from Vatican I is found alongside the doctrine of the collegial structure of Church ministry. The second chapter of that same constitution on the people of God reflects a *communio* ecclesiology, whereas the third chapter outlines a hierarchical ecclesiology. As Ernest Henau writes, these are not compromises in the negative sense of the word. Henau calls for understanding in the difficult and delicate task of realizing simultaneously two intentions which seem incompatible at first sight, namely renewal and continuity.[19]

Understanding this is easier for the theologian than for the canon lawyer. The theologian tends to sublimate the contradiction with lyrical fervor, transcending it by what he or she might call an enriching completion, or a higher synthesis. The canon lawyer sees things differently. The canonist scowls as soon as he or she is confronted with absolute papal power on the one hand (Canon 331) and the obligations and rights of all the Christian faithful on the other (Canons 208-223), norms which come close to

---

[19] E. Henau, *De kerk: instrument en teken van heil*, Leuven, 1989, 32.

general human rights. The law is often a pitiless mirror. Rhetoric must give way to the simple logic of the principle of scarcity.

Theological ambivalence, however, provides one more argument for a view of law which allows several angles and levels of approach in equal manner. Even if one should hold the view that the law can, in an almost linear way, be deduced from the underlying theological mass of ideas, this view immediately becomes relative if those theological roots diverge among themselves. The law reclaims a bit of its liberty, causing the actual view of the law to become more important. This paves the way for different approaches, providing more room for structures for dialogue, and for a jurisprudence which develops gradually.

Conclusion

This chapter was aimed at drawing attention to the role of law and the view of law within the dicussion on human rights in the Church. Far too often the discussion around this subject remains too theological. However, as has been pointed out, the law is far from a neutral element in all of this. For one thing, there are a great many divergent legal traditions. Canon law is primarily based upon the Western continental tradition. However, from a theological point of view it might as well have been the Anglo-American tradition supporting the system, with perhaps surprising consequences in practice. But even on the basis of the present Western continental tradition, there is quite a bit of room for a variety of approaches, certainly in view of a wavering underlying theology. Whether the present Code is looked upon from a macro, meso or micro point of view, theological orthodoxy has nothing to do with it. In this field the three angles of approach are legitimate. The present discussion is a juridical one. It is far more exciting than one would expect.

CHAPTER III

THE GENESIS AND PRESENT SITUATION OF HUMAN RIGHTS IN THE CHURCH

History

Human rights as such are a recent phenomenon in the Church. They are absent for the most part in the history of canon law. In the 1917 Code of Canon Law an indirect reference appears in Canon 87 which specifies what constitutes a "person" in the Church. The concept of "person" refers here to a person with all the rights and obligations of a Christian. The 1917 Code does not say what this means exactly. It would be useless to look for some list of rights and obligations. Of course, this does not mean that these do not exist, but clarifying what that term meant was not seen as a priority.

In 1950 a congress was held at the Gregorian University in Rome on subjective rights and their protection in canon law. One of the speakers was the Leuven professor, Willy Onclin. He requested a clearer definition and greater protection of the subjective rights which belong to all the faithful. In this period that was certainly a revolutionary proposition. For Onclin, basic rights were certainly not distant, unknown concepts, because he also taught Introduction to Law courses in the Faculty of Law.

General interest in the issue of basic rights in the Church cannot be found until about the time of the Second Vatican Council.[20] Then everything changed very quickly. Why? Cardinal Castillo Lara cites four factors. On one side there was the influence of the Universal Declaration on Human Rights. Secondly, and more specifically, the doctrine of the Second Vatican Council played a role by giving special attention to human dignity and respect for each person. Thirdly, there was the breakthrough of the idea of the People of God in ecclesiology. And, finally, the recognition of the radical equality of all Christians exerted influence on the discussion.[21]

In the period between the end of the Council and the promulgation of the Code of Canon Law in 1983, canon lawyers carried on an extensive reflection on the theme of basic rights in the Church. Are they necessary? What is their legal foundation? What would a concrete catalogue of rights look like?

Concerning the legal foundation, we can distinguish three currents with a number of variations linked to each one, which might be described as juridical, ecclesiological and anthropological.

Schematically expressed, the juridical theory begins from the idea that civil basic rights can function as a guideline to lead to basic rights in the Church. This does not fundamentally alter the existing situation. It would be necessary to make certain adjustments related to the unique nature of the Church, but no fundamental rethinking is required. Alvaro del Portillo for example, the former prelate of Opus Dei, can be situated on this line. He argues that the roots of human rights can be found in the

---

[20] J. Kremsmair, "Grundrechte im Codex Iuris Canonici 1983", *Österreichisches Archiv für Kirchenrecht* 42 (1993) 50.
[21] R.J. Castillo Lara, "Some Reflections on the Rights and Duties of the Christian Faithful", *Studia Canonica* 20 (1986) 10.

dignity of the human person. In the same way the rights of Christians flow from their dignity.[22] Therefore, there is no essential difference in nature between human rights and the rights of the Christian. Indeed, one might even speak of an analogical foundation.

The authors who defend the ecclesiological theory believe that the issue of basic rights in the Church must be authentically ecclesiological from the beginning. An approach which does not follow this path is in danger of building a theory of basic rights which is not well integrated in the system of law as a whole, a system which in fact has very clear ecclesiological roots.

The most prominent defender of this position is Paul Hinder.[23] Basic rights must be different in the Church than elsewhere, according to this author. The main issue is not the individual who must defend herself or himself against the authorities, but instead the *communio* of all believers. Moreover, what is at stake here is not the person simply as a social being, but the person in his or her totality, that is to say, in all dimensions of his or her existence. The influence exerted over that individual existence by law must be complementary, not totalitarian. Hinder does not see basic rights in terms of natural law. One cannot simply translate natural law into positive law. In any case, does an indicative automatically constitute an imperative? Nor does the author believe in pure fundamental rights. Hinder instead sees basic rights as functional — they help to make the *communio* operative in practice. The structure of this communio is governed by

---

[22] A. del Portillo, "Ius associationis et associationes fidelium iuxta Concilii Vaticani II doctrinam", *Ius Canonicum* 8 (1968) 5-28.

[23] P. Hinder, *Grundrechte in der Kirche: Eine Untersuchung zur Begründung der Grundrechte in der Kirche*, Fribourg, 1977.

three elements: *das Wort* (the kerygmatic element), *das Sakrament* (the sacramental element), and *die apostolische Sukzession* (the apostolic element.) Hinder concludes his book with a catalogue of basic rights which he derives from each of these elements. From the kerygmatic aspect comes, among other things, the right to hear the Word of God and the right to communication. The sacramental aspect implies, among other things, the right to charity and to the sacraments. The apostolic element is the origin of the right to share in the work of the ordained clergy, the right of clergy to be heard, and so forth. So Hinder does, in fact, maintain the notion of basic rights, but gives them an entirely new meaning in the wake of his ecclesiological theory — a Copernican revolution in comparison with the thought patterns of those inspired by the juridical model.

Johannes Neumann defends a standpoint which straddles the gap between the juridical and the theological theories.[24] He draws a very sharp distinction between human rights enshrined in canon law which are recognized and guaranteed by the Church, on the one hand, and, on the other hand, the fundamental rights of Christians which are derived from the Gospel. He is fully aware of the large gap between divine inspiration and human law. Neumann finds that there is insufficient research done on the question of which guidelines are inherently necessary to permit basic rights to function within the Church in a meaningful manner. The author insists appropriately on that ecclesiological touchstone, which nevertheless is no more than that: a moment of serious ecclesiological med-

---

[24] J. Neumann, *Menschenrechte auch in der Kirche?*, Zurich/Cologne/Einsiedeln, 1976.

itation within a system which in essence is juridical. Neumann does not accept any approach which takes the New Testament as its starting point, because it contains insufficient "political" directives to lead to solid legislation.

Besides the juridical and the theological theories, there is in addition a more anthropological approach. Human rights must be accepted on anthropological grounds. Basic rights in the Church can be articulated in the light of the Church's self-awareness, according to Knut Walf, but the Church is not allowed to create these rights out of nothing, as it were.[25]

Thus, in legal doctrine we find three main theories, juridical, ecclesiological and anthropological, along with the necessary nuances, built up piece by piece. Human rights in the Church grew into a topic of interest especially during the 1970's. The bibliography which can be found at the end of this book gives testimony to that.

In the meantime, legislators were not idle. In Rome lengthy deliberations over the promulgation of a legal constitution for the Church, a *Lex Ecclesiae Fundamentalis*, which would contain, among other things, provision for basic rights, took place. Although a veritable mountain of preparatory work was done, primarily by Professor Onclin, the constitution never saw the light of day. The project ran up against a storm of protest. The arguments against the work included the following:

a) The L.E.F. (*Lex Ecclesiae Fundamentalis*) is an innovation that breaks with a long tradition and which, in addition, ignores the uniqueness of the Eastern churches.

---

[25] K. Walf, "Die Menschenrechte in der katholischen Kirche", *Diakonia* 5 (1974) 376-388.

b) The L.E.F. is dangerous because it imposes an exclusively Latin interpretation of the Second Vatican Council.

c) The promulgation of the L.E.F. would be unnecessary. The Church never needed a constitution before and does not need one now because there are councils, the texts of the Second Vatican Council, the Gospel and the Word of God: these are the true constitution. Secular societies do need this sort of *lex fundamentalis* because they arise from a social contract, while the Church is the result of a divine calling.

d) The L.E.F. is a complicated and massive document which could be a hindrance to ecumenical dialogue.

So there was no constitution for the Church, to the regret of many canon lawyers. But the duties and rights of all Christian believers, originally planned as a subsection in this constitution, did find a home in the 1983 Code of Canon Law, particularly in Canons 208-223, at the beginning of Book II on the People of God. What is striking here is the terminological maneuver: the Code speaks of "obligations and rights of all the Christian faithful," not about human rights, nor about the closely related term fundamental rights. The latter is somewhat suprising since the term "fundamental rights" was still being used during the early phase of the work by the study group *De laicis*, whose reporter was the former prelate of Opus Dei, Alvaro del Portillo. Commentators attribute the fact that it was ultimately thrown out to five factors: the Code does not use the expression; the term connotes a more individualistic struggle by the human subject against the state; a member of the faith community does not exist before the Church exists; the term "fundamental" is not entirely clear; and the list of rights is not complete. These five arguments do not seem totally convincing, and J.A. Coriden refutes them with no difficulty.[26] But the discussion does illustrate a fear of rights which can become so fundamental that even the Church authorities cannot surmount it. "Obligations and rights" sounds much more reassuring. Later in this book I will use the terms in tandem with each other: human rights, fundamental rights, basic rights, obligations and rights of all Christian faithful ... the reader will run into all of these.

The Legal Nature of the Obligations and Rights of All Christian Faithful

Before examining the content of Canons 208-223 in the following chapter, it will be helpful to take a look at the package as a whole, the collection of the duties and rights of all Christians.

The first thing which strikes a civil lawyer is the somewhat eccentric formulation, obligations and rights of all Christians, with the obligations first. What could be the reason for this?[27]

In a certain sense (but certainly not the primary sense), a general skepticism regarding the existence of subjective

[26] J.A. Coriden, "Reflections on Canonical Rights", in J.H. Provost and K. Walf, eds., *Ius sequitur vitam: Studies in Canon Law Presented to P.J.M. Huizing*, Leuven, 1991, 33-34. In a footnote he cites the publications of his opponents, namely Cardinal Rosalio Castillo Lara and Msgr. Eugenio Corecco, Bishop of Lugano.

[27] See in this regard J. Provost, "Freedom of Conscience and Religion: Human Rights in the Church", in Fédération Internationale des Universités Catholiques, ed., *Culture chrétienne et droits de l'homme*, Brussels/Louvain-la-Neuve, 1991, 50-53.

rights in the Church has played a role. One cannot make demands of the Church in the same way as in civil society, according to this theory, because the Church is the Body of Christ, the People of God, and a mere creature cannot claim rights from his or her Creator. While a number of Protestant thinkers subscribed to this idea,[28] it never got off the ground in the Catholic church.

Another interpretative model is more helpful. According to this line of reasoning — followed by Paul Hinder and others — obligations have priority over rights. The starting point is the person's state of life or position. Following from that one can ascertain which obligations pertain to it. Only thereafter can one work out whether rights can also be linked to these obligations. Duties and rights (*doveri-diritti*) are presented as an inseparable pair. One cannot say that this approach is objectionable per se, but it certainly seems voluntaristic. In addition the picture is not always true. Take, for example, although it is not formulated in the Code, the right to life. Which obligations have priority in this case? The obligation to be born?

But the formulation is what it is. Sixteen canons fall under the title "obligations and rights of all Christian believers." And while the epithets fundamental rights, basic rights or human rights are denied them, they do indeed concern specifications which, in terms of content, can be placed along the same lines.

The question at this point is, what is the intent of these basic rights? Is the juridical theory employed? Was a choice made for an ecclesiological approach along the lines of Paul Hinder? Or is the legislator following an anthropological vision of fundamental rights? A glance at

---

[28] J.H. Lochmann, "Les Églises réformées et la théologie des 'droits de l'homme'", *Revue Théologique de Louvain* 10 (1979) 348-352.

the canons shows that this kind of choice was avoided. There exists no clear theory of basic rights which permeates the whole doctrine which lies at the foundation of the catalogue presented by the Code in Canons 208-223. Diverse sources of inspiration contributed to the colorful collection of obligations and rights such as they are presently formulated.

A number of stipulations are clearly ecclesiologically oriented; they remain typical for Church life and have hardly any link with secular legal conventions on human rights. I am thinking of, for example, the duty to lead a holy life (Canon 210), the duty and the right to commit oneself to the spread of the divine Gospel (Canon 211), the right to celebrate the liturgy following one's own approved rite (Canon 214), the right to a Christian education (Canon 217), the freedom of choice in a state of life (Canon 219), and the obligation to contribute to the needs of the Church (Canon 222).

These stipulations dovetail nicely with the theory of Paul Hinder, more specifically with the three basic elements around which he constructs his catalogue of rights, namely word, sacrament and apostolic succession. In this schema the right to a Christian education primarily has to do with the word; the right found in Canon 213 to receive assistance through the sacraments, with sacrament; and obedience to the ordained pastors who represent Christ (Canon 212) with the apostolic succession.

However, in addition to these theologically inspired rights there are others as well which overlap with, or run closely parallel to, the fundamental rights which regularly appear in civil lists. That is the case for the principle of equality (Canon 208), the right to free expression of opinion (Canon 212, par. 3), the right to form associations

(Canon 215), the right to a good reputation and to privacy (Canon 220), the right to claim one's rights in accord with the law and the principle of "no punishment without law" (Canon 221). Hinder's model applies less clearly to this type of right. In this way the Church implicitly recognizes the existence within the Church of rights which do not proceed exclusively from the ecclesial context, and which cannot be supported exclusively on theological grounds. This could point in the direction of a vision of human rights as an anthropological given, in the line of Knut Walf. But the basis for this line of thought could just as well be found in the application of civil human rights conventions as a source of inspiration.

Besides the more theologically and the more juridically inspired rights there is a third category, one which can be interpreted in two ways with very different consequences.

I am thinking here, for example, of the otherwise carefully formulated Canon 208 which expresses the principle of equality: "In virtue of their rebirth in Christ there exists among all the Christian faithful a true equality with regard to dignity and the activity whereby all cooperate in the building up of the Body of Christ in accord with each one's own condition and function." The phrasing is vague, but at least the principle of equality is formulated in the Code of Canon Law.

In his analysis of this provision, the late Marcel Diet, a dynamic Flemish canonist who taught in Germany, demonstrated that Canon 208 is theological in nature, and that one cannot draw practical juridical conclusions from it.[29] He argued that the equality in Canon 208 relates back

---

[29] M. Diet, "Die Gleichheit aller Gläubigen in der Kirche. Zu Kanon 208 des CIC 1983", *Theologie der Gegenwart* 31 (1988) 113-121.

to the Second Vatican Council, specifically to the Dogmatic Constitution on the Church *Lumen Gentium*, nr. 32.
In this regard he notes correctly that this passage in the
Council documents has only a theological and not a
juridical meaning. But then he makes a dangerous leap in
proposing that, due to its origin, Canon 208 is a purely
theological statement and is therefore juridically irrele-
vant. His main argument, which he develops in a footnote, is purely linguistic. Canon 208 determines that there
exists a genuine equality among all Christians. But that
existence is expressed by the Latin word *viget*, in the
indicative. That means that this equality already exists; it
is no longer waiting to be realized. Hence, the provision
is purely theological. If the text were juridical, according
to Diet, then it would undoubtedly have read *vigeat*, a
subjunctive which contains not so much a statement as a
mission. This, of course, is splitting hairs. Article 10 of
the Belgian Constitution states: "All Belgians are equal
before the law." It does not say that they must be equal.
Nobody doubts the juridical character of this article of the
Constitution in any case.

It is unnecessary to add that Diet's reasoning, if followed, leads to an interpretation by which the principle of
equality is simply a decoration, devoid of all real significance in the system of law.

Another sharp illustration of the difference in meaning
and in legal consequences between a theological and a
juridical approach can be found in Canon 213. This provision reads as follows: "The Christian faithful have the
right to receive assistance from the sacred pastors out of
the spiritual goods of the Church, especially the word of
God and the sacraments." A double interpretation is possible. One can find here a declaration of a theological

principle based on *Sacrosanctum Concilium*, nr. 9, *Lumen Gentium*, nr. 7 and *Presbyterorum Ordinis*, nr. 9, and one can rejoice over the existence of a canonical expression of the line of thought developed by the Second Vatican Council. But one can also insist upon a juridical implementation of Canon 213. If all Christians enjoy a genuine right to the assistance of ordained pastors, would there not be a corresponding duty on the part of the hierarchy to set the criteria for ordination such that the intended assistance can in fact be given? What would happen in that case with compulsory celibacy, since no one can assert that this belongs to divine law and is thus untouchable? Canonists such as H. Eysink and R. Huysmans appear to adopt a more juridical line of reasoning. This type of interpretation suddenly makes the fine, gentle Canon 213 into an explosive legal stipulation. It seems clear to me that the legislators did not intend it this way, but, as we already saw, we must not forget that, according to Canon 17, the intention of the legislator does not play a role in the interpretation of laws whenever the words of the law are clear. And these are clear, to the degree that words in themselves can be clear. So the discussion is not concerned with the text of the law itself, but rather with the question of whether the canon in question should be considered as a right or as a theological reflection.

My personal preference is for a juridical interpretation of laws, for two very simple reasons. The fact that Canons 208 through 223 can be found in a Code of Canon Law indicates that a juridical interpretation is to be preferred to a theological. Whenever one is confronted with a rule of law one must keep in mind the ancient maxim *potius ut valeat quam ut pereat* (better to stand firm than to perish). This implies that if there are two ways to read a certain law, it is better to choose a reading which accords a law real significance and does not render it meaningless. Indeed, if it were only intended to be leisure reading, the Code of Canon Law lacks a certain dramatic tension and literary refinement.

Here ends a short description of the obligations and rights of all Christians in the present Code of Canon Law. After a long period of discussion, they were taken up under this designation in the present Code. The text as it stands now is not the result of a carefully determined, brilliantly clear fundamental vision. But when a choice must be made betwen a juridical or a theological interpretation of the law, it would be better to choose the former.

The fourth chapter will contain a catalogue and an analysis of the obligations and rights as set out in Canons 208-223. This reading will pay considerable attention to the micro-level described in the previous chapter, and thus to the experiential world and the sense of law held by the ordinary Christian: ordinary Christians who realize that a great deal can be attained on the basis of the open norms of law proposed by the Code.

CHAPTER IV

AN OVERVIEW OF THE OBLIGATIONS AND RIGHTS OF ALL CHRISTIAN FAITHFUL

Catalogue

The following obligations and rights of all the Christian faithful can be found in the Code of Canon Law:

* the principle of equality (Canon 208);
* the obligation to maintain communion with the Church (Canon 209);
* the duty to lead a holy life and to promote the growth of the Church (Canon 210);
* the duty and the right to work so that the divine message of salvation may spread over the whole world (Canon 211);
* the duty to obey the sacred pastors and the right to freedom of expression (Canon 212);
* the right to receive assistance from the sacred pastors out of the spiritual goods of the Church (Canon 213);
* the right to worship in one's own rite and to one's own form of spiritual life (Canon 214);
* the freedom of association and to hold meetings (Canon 215);
* the right to promote apostolic activity, with a few restrictions on the use of the name Catholic (Canon 216);

* the right to a Christian education (Canon 217);
* freedom of research for those engaged in sacred disciplines (Canon 218);
* the right to choose a state of life free from any coercion (Canon 219);
* the right to a good reputation and to privacy (Canon 220);
* the right to defend oneself, and to an equitable trial; the right not to be punished except according to the law (Canon 221);
* the obligation to provide for the needs of the Church and to promote social justice (Canon 222);
* the duty to take account of the common good of the Church (Canon 223).

Most of these prescriptions probably contain more possibilities than one would think at first glance, even more than the legislators originally wished to write into them. This is typical for human rights. I will investigate three of these in greater detail.

The Principle of Equality

I have already dealt with the way in which Canon 208 recognizes true equality in dignity and activity among all Christians, by means of which each person, in terms of her or his own position and function, cooperates in the building up of the Church.

This provision seems somewhat vague. In the design for the *Lex Ecclesiae Fundamentalis*, Canon 9, inequality on the basis of race, nation, social position and sex was considered unacceptable. In the Code of Canon Law of

1983 these specific prohibitions in regard to discrimination unfortunately disappeared. In addition Canon 208 immediately nuances the principle of equality which the canon itself has just expressed. The phrase, "... in accord with each one's own condition and function" was not originally planned; it was added later and offers considerable possibilities to introduce apparently legitimate differences.

In any case it was already a concern of the authors of the *Lex Ecclesiae Fundamentalis*, a concern which certainly did not diminish among the editors of Canon 208, not to give the impression that equality in the Church has the same character as democratic equality.[30] Perhaps for that reason Canon 208 speaks of *true* equality (*vera aequalitas*), which apparently cannot be associated with everyday equality. How true is true equality? Does it also apply to women?[31] Or is true equality too good to be true? Is it in fact what an ordinary mortal would simply call inequality? Or, to use the language of some officials in the Church, isn't a woman much too noble and exalted a being to be dealt with in terms of ordinary equality, as if she were only a man?

Apart from all these typical canon law questions, we should stop and consider how the concept of equality can be understood in a general juridical way. A distinction can be made among equality before, in and through the law.[32]

[30] See *Communicationes* 12 (1980) 35-36.

[31] On the legal statute of women in the Church, see H. Warnink, "Vrouwen in het canoniek recht", in E. Borgman, B. van Dijk and Th. Salemink, eds., *Recht en onrecht in de rooms-katholieke kerk*, Amersfoort/Leuven, 1989, 73-83.

[32] On this point see L. Ingber, "L'égalité dans la jurisprudence belge", in H. Buch, P. Foriers and C. Perelman, eds., *L'égalité*, Brussels, 1971, I, 4-5.

Equality *before* the law means that everyone in society has a right to respect for their personal dignity, because persons are equal as regards their origin and final end. Hence, no privileges may be attached to the circumstances of one's birth, and the public administration may make no distinctions among citizens as to race, religious conviction or political affiliation. For the rest, equals will be treated equally and unequals treated unequally. The main question here is which categories should be set into that framework. When is it justified to make a distinction?

Equality *in* the law has more to do with the content of certain general norms which grant subjective rights. It seems to be more "equal" than the previous form of equality because it resists making any form of distinction. However, when it permeates all forms of social life it can lead to severe inequalities. Men and women would have to compete in the same tournament for the title at Wimbledon. Indeed, even legally relevant differences would not be taken into account.

Equality *through* the law tries to bring unequal people by unequal treatment to genuine equality. This is the sort of equality that underlies positive discrimination. Women, foreigners and other numerical or social minorities receive preferential treatment to catch up from a history of accumulated disadvantages.

So which of these forms of equality (before, in or through the law) is actually involved in Canon 208? The text of the law says nothing, so in theory any interpretation is possible. At the same time, one may assume that an evolution in the direction of equality before the law has the best chance of being generally accepted. In the pertinent discussion it will be a question of permitting as few forms of legal discrimination as possible to remain legitimate, in spite of the reference in the text of Canon 208 to "each one's own condition and function." Thus, it does not seem acceptable that the difference between man and woman or between lay and cleric should continue to be the starting point for unequal treatment. It can be stated that this idea is shared by very many Catholics today. We have arrived at a stage in which the average Christian would more likely be offended by continuing inequality than by abolishing it. But just as clearly, the sentiments on the part of the hierarchy, at least in their public pronouncements, remain elsewhere. The principle of equality seems to be just one of the ways in which these forms of discrimination can be very seriously called into question.

Freedom of Expression

A glance at Canon 212, par. 3 shows clearly how careful the canonical formulation of the freedom to express one's opinion really is: "In accord with the knowledge, competence and preeminence which they possess, they (the Christian faithful) have the right and even at times a duty to manifest to the sacred pastors their opinion on matters which pertain to the good of the Church, and they have a right to make their opinion known to the other Christian faithful, with due regard for the integrity of faith and morals and reverence toward their pastors, and with consideration for the common good and the dignity of persons."

So what is the scope of this limiting formulation?[33] Naturally it is possible to encourage all sorts of vague

[33] For further details on the freedom of expression and the freedom of theological research in the Church, see R. Torfs, "Estructura eccle-

formulations from a theological point of view, and even to welcome them enthusiastically. It seems better to me to make a short comparison with civil law, specifically the European Convention on Human Rights. Article 10.1 deals with freedom of expression, while article 10.2 sets a number of restrictions. In fact, a comparison of what is meant by freedom of expression under the European Convention with the situation within the Church is very revealing. Two issues in particular come to mind.

First, in the European Convention freedom of expression is cited as just one of the foundations of a democratic society. Taking account of the reservations found in article 10.2, this right is valid not only for information or ideas which would be received positively or which would come across as harmless or indifferent, but also for ideas which might affect, shock or disturb the state or a portion of its population. Dialogue, discussion and freedom of expression have value in themselves.

The concept of freedom of expression looks completely different in canon law. Canon 212, par. 3 proposes that the exercise of freedom of expression must take account of the common good. I would conclude that this implies that, in an ecclesial context, the common good can sometimes be damaged when opinions are expressed. Freedom of expression has an instrumental function.

To sum up, according to the European Convention, the common good is served by freedom of expression; according to canon law, freedom of expression is only permissible when it serves the common good. The two notions are squarely opposed to each other.

siástica y responsabilidad independiente: Reflexiones en torno a los cánones 212 §3 y 218 del CIC 1983", *Revista Española de Derecho Canónico* 47 (1990) 663-694.

Secondly, the European Convention allows exceptions to the principle of freedom of expression only when these are specified in the law. This law must be sufficiently accessible to those subject to the law, and precise enough in its formulation to permit the citizen to invoke it.

This type of guarantee is entirely missing in the approach taken in canon law. The administration itself will determine when freedom of expression becomes inconvenient.

A comparison between the European Convention on Human Rights and the Code of Canon Law shows that the guarantees offered by the former are considerably stronger. But it is not only the comparison which is fascinating. Whoever examines Canon 212, par. 3 in its own right cannot escape a number of pointed questions. A few of these are:

a) Canon 212, par. 3 gives preference to negotiation with the ordained pastors before the issue becomes public. Public debate as a laboratory for new ideas is thus not fully recognized. In American public life things are markedly different, but, even in Western Europe, open discussion in the society over fundamental political options is gaining in importance. However, Canon 212, par. 3 seems to lend indirect support to, for example, a number of Flemish bishops who complain that Christians are fighting out all sorts of conflicts with Church authorities in the media. Does Canon 212, par. 3 in fact forbid an appeal to public opinion when all other possibilities are exhausted? I do not think so. Perhaps the obligation first to appeal to the ordained pastors entails an obligation on the part of those authorities not only to take formal notice of an expressed opinion, but to really listen to it. The appeal to the media needs to be seen in a larger context in any case, in which all the possibilities to permit subjects currently under discussion within the Church to be heard in more than just a formal manner must be investigated.

b) Canon 212, par. 3 stipulates that the right to express one's opinion is also sometimes a duty. But doesn't this raise questions about the case of the subservient individual whose silence is the key to his or her success? Is such a person now to be subject to sanction? Isn't he or she now required to speak out?

c) In expressing their opinions Christians must take account of personal human dignity. Does this imply that one must exercise more caution in regard to representatives of the hierarchy because they have more dignity? Or does the principle of equality in Canon 208 apply? Or could one suggest that, to the degree that someone exercises more important official functions, this person is better able to withstand critique?[34]

There are questions enough, and not all of them purely rhetorical. They do indicate the difficulties involved in giving a precise form to fundamental rights, which are by definition formulated in a vague manner. Their contours are filled in continuously through legal interpretation. Because independent courts of law are absent from the Church we have a problem here. At the moment the concrete interpretation of these rights depends to a large extent on administrative practice. The Cardinal Archbishop of Brussels, for example, when dealing with an

---

[34] This last notion was (in a civil context) the position of the European Court for Human Rights in Strasbourg, in a case dating from 8 July 1986 (Lingens), *Publ. Cour.*, series A vol. 103, p. 26, nr. 42 and 43.

outspoken priest, made a distinction between the latter's right to express his opinions in his capacity as an individual believer and his obligations as a parish priest. That is one possible interpretation.[35] Nevertheless, however hesitant the formulation, and however abundant the number of exceptions might be, there is a limit to the boundaries that can be placed on the freedom of expression. No one can assert that Canon 212, par. 3 describes freedom of expression in such a way that it amounts to an obligation to keep silent.

Freedom of Theological Research

The freedom of theological research, expressed in Canon 218, belongs to the most discussed legal provisions in the present Code: "Those who are engaged in the sacred disciplines enjoy a lawful freedom of inquiry and of prudently expressing their opinions on matters in which they have expertise, while observing a due respect for the magisterium of the Church."

In contrast to the freedom of expression, the freedom of theological research has very little direct link with civil law. As a result, a comparison on this point is impossible. Canon 218 does have a solid theological foundation based on the pastoral constitution *Gaudium et Spes*, nr. 62. It is probably not necessary to point to the delicate character of freedom of theological research. Clearly, anxiety about the threat to orthodoxy, which already gives a negative cast to the idea of basic

---

[35] This distinction was not made in the case of Bishop Gaillot of Evreux, France, in January 1995. See ten articles on this issue in *Revue de droit canonique* 45 (1995) 75-162.

rights in the opinion of many Church leaders, is every-where.

The question of who enjoys freedom of theological research can be answered relatively easily. It concerns persons who apply themselves to the sacred sciences, and in areas in which they have expertise. A positive correlation exists between expertise and freedom of research. Perhaps the opposite would have been more appropriate since it is more often the genuine experts rather than the slick tacticians who get embroiled in conflict.

The closing words of Canon 218 are more open to discussion: "... while observing a due respect for the magisterium of the Church."

There are different types of magisterium. As far as the infallible magisterium is concerned, there are not many possibilities left to the theologian. Canon 749 averts to a purely passive acceptance relating to the infallible magisterium. However, concerning the noninfallible magisterium, which covers the vast majority of cases, there is, of course, more freedom. Certainly, Canon 750 remains strict concerning all that is contained in the written word of God or in tradition. However, according to Canon 752 there is no assent of faith necessary when it comes to the more common ordinary teaching of the pope or the bishops, but only a religious respect of intellect and will. There is no agreement on what this demand means. Some authors assign an interpretation which is all but suffocating. Ladislas Örsy, for example, gives religious respect of intellect and will a rather dynamic coloring. He does this by means of considerations which leave strictly legal territory behind. He attaches a great deal of importance to research, to the process of "faith seeking understanding", *fides quaerens intellectum*. Whenever insufficient consensus exists concerning this investigation, *obsequium* in Canon 752 can involve nothing more than respectfully listening to, and reflecting upon, what has been officially handed on.[36]

More stringent interpretations are also possible, of course, but it quickly becomes clear that the exact evaluation of freedom of theological research, its elasticity and its limits is a highly nuanced undertaking. In any case, there is more room than one would think. A gap exists between a difference of opinion with the magisterium on one hand, and heresy on the other. One does not simply stumble by accident into heresy. That appears crystal clear, for example, in the position of the International Theological Commission in Rome. They are of the opinion that a difference of ideas must be rooted in a genuine respect for the magisterium, even when one absolutely cannot agree on a certain point. They also recall how the classic rules in the case of heresy require "obstinacy" on the part of the accused theologian. That is present if he or she refuses every discussion to clarify their opinion on the point which is opposed to the faith, which amounts to refusing dialogue. The fact of heresy can only be confirmed with reference to all the hermeneutical rules relating to dogma and theological qualifications.[37]

All of the foregoing indicates that setting material limits to the freedom of theological research is not easy. Much depends upon the way in which a certain opinion is formulated. Respect and fair play seem to carry at least as much weight as content-related discussions on magis-

---

[36] L. Örsy, "Reflections on the Text of a Canon", in *Dissent in the Church*, New York/Mahwah, 1988, 231-249, especially 232-233.

[37] "Theses de Magisterii Ecclesiastici et Theologiae ad invicem relatione", *Gregorianum* 57 (1976) 549-563.

terium. Or, in other words, *c'est le ton qui fait la chanson*. Carefully weighed propositions formulated elegantly and fairly will be more easily accepted than violent outbursts which do not contribute much on the level of content. Even more: the hierarchical authorities can justify such a distinction in treatment on the basis of Canon 218, because the obedience required is certainly not a question of content alone, but of attitude, of form, and of social graces.

It is at once fascinating and paradoxical that the question of form suddenly acquires such prominence. What is at stake here is an issue that is of vital importance to the church authorities, namely, the freedom of theological research and its potentially frightening consequences for orthodoxy (at least as far as the authorities are concerned). Just at this juncture, the question of form, the formal aspect, the way in which something is said is accorded prominence. Ought this not cause us to pause and reflect? Is there something more at stake here than the immediate problem? When it really counts, "in the heat of the night", so to speak, form acquires a very important place alongside content. When the going gets tough, form becomes the arbiter. Critical reflection on Canon 218, that is to say, consideration of the canon in its own right, leads to an impasse. The issue of where precisely the teaching authority limits the freedom of theological research is dependent on theological research into the scope of the teaching authority. Pessimists will regard this as a circular argument; optimists can just as justifiably look upon it as a case of dialectical fertilization. In any case, the impossibility of overcoming this tension simply in terms of content, leads to renewed attention to form.

Concluding Considerations and Guidelines

In this chapter, after summarizing the obligations and rights of all Christians, an attempt was made to investigate three of them more deeply. This never led at any time to a sharp delineation of the basic right in question. With regard to the principle of equality, freedom of expression and freedom of theological research, a number of questions remained unanswered. It was clear, however, that while, in all three instances, legislators wanted to build in maximum protection against too much latitude for basic rights, the present formulation of these laws still offers a wide range of possibilities. Nevertheless, a possibility is nothing more than that. Something may come of it, but then again something may not.

This brings us to one final remark concerning the considerations developed in this chapter. They are not yet the stuff of reality. Are we dealing here with a gimmick devised by an ivory-tower scholar to display the brighter side of the existing rules? That danger is not inconceivable. It is certainly the case that a carefully-framed strategy is needed if the existing law is to yield the hidden possibilities it contains. One might regret this. Does one now need a finely-tuned strategic sense to keep afloat in the church? In any case, I fear that little can be achieved with respect to the issue of fundamental rights in the church without at least some sensitivity to strategy. In the following chapter, we will attempt to sketch the beginnings of a strategic approach.

CHAPTER V

TOWARD A THOROUGH CULTURE OF LAW

Rowing Upstream

If we want to see something come of human rights in the Church, we cannot be satisfied simply with optimistic descriptions of the existing laws. Empty flourishes of praise give no results. We must seek out ways to struggle against the anti-juridical mentality which still dominates the Church. The false opposition elucidated above between law and love offers an illustration of this negative vision. But, of course, there is much more. How often do we see attempts to introduce techniques from civil law into the internal church discussion shot down? Civil law has nothing to do with the Church, the story goes, because the Church is completely different. Civil legal mechanisms simply do not work here. But one forgets, deliberately and with premeditation, to explain just which mechanisms really have proven their effectiveness in the context of our Church.

It is urgent that we begin to work on building up within the Church a culture of law. However, first a number of prejudices must be overcome. There does exist a gigantic difference between a lawsuit and a world war. And there is not necessarily an all-consuming hatred between the *dramatis personae* behind the scenes of every legal conflict brought to trial. Obviously every lawyer knows this.

However, in the Church, arguments still need to be adduced to demonstrate that a legal system which works well is liveable. Up to the present a spontaneous trust in the magical power of the mantle of love still predominates. So how can we begin to develop a culture of law? Perhaps only by gradually building up an atmosphere of acceptance. A gentle legal structure can very slowly make its way into the life of the Church, writing a story in which, after awhile, its presence becomes self-evident, a story which is reassuring.

It seems to me that jurisprudence plays a crucial role in all of this. Precisely because, by definition, it has been developed as a result of very concrete cases, jurisprudence will never appear as revolutionary, threatening or destructive. The story of law cannot be more beautifully written than in the uniform handwriting of jurisprudence.

In this regard we should not forget to mention Ronald Dworkin, a man from the Anglo-American legal world and thus exceptionally familiar with the potential of a carefully balanced jurisprudence. He does not see this as a rival to the legal text. According to Dworkin, the dichotomy between finding and inventing law is a false one.[38] It is not a case of one or the other. Dworkin believes much more in a consideration of law as a *chain of law*. He illustrates his standpoint by means of a comparison with the writing of a *chain novel*. A group of authors write a book together, in the sense that one writer follows the other and begins from what has already been written. When an author wants to properly discharge his or her task, the author will take account of everything

---

[38] R. Dworkin, *Law's Empire*, London, 1986, 228.

which precedes in an intelligent and responsible manner. In this occupation various decisions must be made.

On the one hand, it is important that the coherence and integrity of the overall story be maintained; on the other hand, one must take account of the more substantial limitations imposed by the developing story-line. This possibility for conflict and mutual influence between what is textual and what is substantial has distinguished the work of the *chain novelist* from that of more independent authors.

Dworkin illustrates the fact that one's own contribution is progressively conditioned by the developing text, by means of Charles Dickens' *A Christmas Carol*, the world-famous story in which the hardened capitalist, Scrooge, who oppresses his workers, gradually repents. At the beginning of the story a *chain novelist* can find a number of possible story lines. Perhaps Scrooge himself is just an irredeemably bad person. Perhaps he has simply been perverted by the false values of a merciless capitalism which happens to shape his world. As the story unfolds and develops it becomes harder to depict certain hypotheses in a credible way. Scrooge can hardly be depicted as thoroughly bad when he converts his way of life in thought and deed.

A lovely story. So what does this have to do with the protection of fundamental rights in a canonical situation? First, it seems that the role played by the legal text is not that of a magic pill. This is even more so whenever the text is not understandable enough to allow it to be applied to concrete situations using purely logical mechanisms. But there is another important element which comes to the fore in Dworkin's analysis: law and a culture of law, grow. The text and the will of the original legislator are not everything. Or, as Ronald Dworkin himself writes, the process of reflection begins right now, and only connects with the past insofar as it seems necessary or helpful from a contemporary perspective.

Another argument which pleads for a dynamic culture of law is the way in which basic rights are dealt with in civil law. Here are two examples. The principle of equality as formulated in the 1831 Belgian Constitution, article 10, was not able to prevent women from being seriously discriminated against on all levels of society. It was even considered necessary to introduce a number of specific laws to legislate equality for women in different areas. Thus, a woman can be a lawyer only since 1922, a judge since 1948, and a notary public since 1950.[39] Nevertheless no one today would consider a prohibition on women in these professions to be compatible with the principle of equality, and that would also be confirmed in a court of law. The principle of equality is still the principle of equality, but its content has changed, sometimes imperceptibly and sometimes with a few shocks. It is perhaps not too bold to postulate that, to the degree that a culture of law is more finely developed, evolution will take place in a more harmonious way.

On the basis of the foregoing it seems clear that the time is ripe to work systematically toward a culture of law in the Church, a culture in which basic rights have an eminent contribution to make. Long-distance hiking boots are not the best equipment for this undertaking. The steps will have to be small and measured. Concretely and practically speaking, the battle will be joined on two fronts.

---

[39] See respectively Law 7 April 1922, *Moniteur belge*, 21 April 1922; Law 21 February 1948, *Moniteur belge*, 5 March 1948; Law 1 March 1950, *Moniteur belge*, 15 March 1950.

First, clarity is necessary with respect to the exact statute of the obligations and rights of all Christians within the current Code of Canon Law. The second task involves determining how the position of basic rights can be assured and made practicable. In this stage the demand for adequate legal procedures comes unavoidably to the fore.

Statute of the Obligations and Rights of All Christians

The key question with regard to the obligations and the rights of all Christians, as proclaimed in Canons 208 through 223 is, are these formally superior to other provisions in the Code? Or to put it another way, whenever there is a dispute between a basic right and a stipulation elsewhere in the Code, does the basic right rank a step higher or not? Must the other stipulation be interpreted in the light of the basic right? Or must one, on the contrary, in the line of Canon 20 and the maxim *lex specialis derogat generali* (the particular law revokes the general), presume that the particular law has precedence over the general?

The consequences are enormous. Take, for example, Canon 208. As we have already mentioned, this law stipulates, with a number of restrictions, that there is a true equality in dignity and activity among all Christians. If this canon has no formal superiority, if legally it is no more influential than any other canon in the Code, then on the basis of the priority of the particular law it cannot go against specific definitions which make discrimination against women and lay people, for example, possible. Canon 229, par. 3 states very concretely that lay persons, allowing for the prescriptions concerning the required suitability, are capable of receiving from legitimate eccle-

siastical authorities a mandate to teach the sacred sciences. If this canon were interpreted in the light of the
principle of equality, then in the case of a choice between
a clerical and a lay candidate, the best one would be
appointed. Indeed, the principle of equality makes the
appointment of a lay person compulsory if the lay person
is the best qualified candidate. If one separates the two
provisions, then nothing would prevent a less qualified
cleric from being appointed in preference to a better qualified lay person. The theoretical right of the lay person as
described in Canon 229, par. 3 remains in force and so
does the principle of equality as an abstract principle.

A second example illustrates just as clearly the importance of requiring the formal supremacy of basic rights.
In Canon 1741 five reasons are summarized for which a
pastor could legitimately be removed from his parish. The
third one reads, "loss of good reputation among upright
and good parishioners or aversion to the pastor which are
foreseen as not ceasing in a short time." This definition
offers food for thought. One question concerns just what
sort of heroic deeds are necessary to be able to enjoy the
status of an "upright and good parishioner." But, more
importantly, there is the conclusion that the loss of one's
reputation need not necessarily be based upon hard facts
to be legally relevant. Rumors, for example, can be
enough. What counts is not why one has lost one's good
name, but the fact in itself. None of this sounds very
good. But the provision can be explained with reference
to a long ecclesial tradition in which public opinion was
taken seriously and great juridical relevance was attributed to the concept of *scandalum*.

Canon 220 seems to bring this train of thought to a
screeching halt: "No one is permitted to damage unlaw-

fully the good reputation which another person enjoys nor to violate the right of another person to protect his or her own privacy." There is undoubtedly tension between Canon 220 and Canon 1741 to the extent that the latter also covers unfounded rumors. If Canon 220 is formally superior, Canon 1741 must be explained in such a way that a pastor whose good reputation is unlawfully damaged cannot be dismissed from his parish. If both legal provisions stand on the same level, the preference would have to be given to Canon 1741, which is more specific.

The two examples cited above, which are based respectively on the principle of equality and the right to a good reputation as basic rights, make clear the significance of the problem. I think that the discussion over the hierarchy of legal provisions is essential for the future of basic rights in the Church. If one accepts their formal supremacy, then basic rights will soon form a leaven permeating the whole system. If one does not do that, then they remain gratuitous declarations of principle which will be pushed aside in any discussion. There will always be good-sounding reasons to consider the application of fundamental rights unnecessary in a particular situation.

Opponents of the formal authority of the obligations and rights of all Christians can naturally add that one cannot speak of a formal preeminence for provisions which are found in the middle of the Code. Why would Canons 208 to 223 need to be superior to Canon 224, for example? If these provisions were incorporated into a *Lex Ecclesiae Fundamentalis*, in a constitution for the Church, as originally intended, then their preferential status would be undeniable. But when the plans for such a constitution were scrapped, the basic rights which would have been taken up into it, lost their authority, it might be said.

I can hardly suggest that this argument holds no water at all, but it does fall short. First, the title "The Obligations and Rights of all the Christian Faithful" figures above Canons 208-223. That gives them a sort of halo. They rise above ordinary legal provisions elsewhere, in process law for example, such as the canons which deal with the removal of pastors. The failure to recognize their formal superiority leads to problems of a systematic nature. So, for example, Canon 229, par. 3 and the possibility for lay persons to receive a teaching appointment in the sacred sciences stands under the title, "The Obligations and Rights of the Lay Christian Faithful." This stipulation would then have to be completely disconnected from the principle of equality, which belongs to "The Obligations and Rights of all the Christian Faithful." If one holds that there is perfect mutual independence between both categories of law, then one can make peace with a Code in which each strand hangs separately, which lacks all systematization, and amounts to nothing more than a store of totally disconnected rules. This is no longer a question of law as even a skeleton. It is more a question of law as a necessary evil.

But there is a still more important and simple argument for the recognition of the formal superiority of Canons 208-223, namely their complete uselessness if this superiority is denied. Their practical relevance is then, indeed, absolutely zero. Based on these premises, basic rights, by definition vague and abstract, would be powerless over other concrete provisions. The legislator could not have intended this. Support for the preference for the formal superiority of obligations and rights, exactly as in the case of the principle of equality, can still be found in the ancient maxim, *potius ut valeat quam ut pereat.* If there are two possible ways to interpret a legal provision, one must choose for a reading by which such a provision has genuine meaning and does not become meaningless.

The formal superiority of Canons 208-223 is not yet an exhausted question. The doctrine of law is only moderately interested in it. The preference is, and certainly was in the past, to write about the juridical statute of altar girls. Be this as it may. In the meantime a canon lawyer who brings to the discipline a warm heart has his or her work cut out in pointing up the necessity of a formal superiority for the obligations and rights of all Christians. This option is a necessity for two reasons: for the sake of the ordinary Christian in the Church, but also for the sake of the dignity and quality of canon law in its entirety.

Protection of Rights

Even if the formal superiority of basic rights becomes more generally accepted, without rules which guarantee its enforceability, the results of this principle will be limited. In the absence of well-balanced procedures, the finest legal stipulations will remain for the most part a dead letter. Now the protection of rights is not the strong point of the Code in any case, which in this area is even weighed down by a lack of consistency. In this way Canon 221, par. 1 affirms, with a certain solemnity, "The Christian faithful can legitimately vindicate and defend the rights which they enjoy in the Church before a competent ecclesiastical court in accord with the norm of law". But the reality is considerably less encouraging. Administrative courts of law, originally planned for the future, were ultimately missing from the CIC 1983.

Canon 221, par. 1 gives the impression that it starts from the assumption that these courts really do exist. It appears at first glance that the legislators lost track of Canon 221, par. 1 at the same time as administrative courts of law. But an explanation which is less humiliating for the legislator is possible. The only legally valid Latin text of Canon 221 speaks of the defense of rights before a competent *forum*, which is broader than a court of law or *tribunal*, a term which was not used. *Forum* means a body or agency, a fairly open concept. And given this meaning, Canon 221, par. 1 can in fact designate a legal procedure such as that which is present in the Code.[40] In case of legal complaints against Church authorities one must first go the way of recourse against administrative decrees (Canons 1732-1739.) After these have been exhausted one can appeal to an administrative court of law, namely the second section of the Apostolic Signature. The address of this court? Rome. In civil law we are used to more proximity.

Is this procedure satisfactory? No. It travels a long and complicated route and is impenetrable to the average Christian. In practice this combination of hierarchical appeal and administrative procedure is almost exclusively set aside for well-experienced veterans of church procedure or quixotic dreamers.

Fortunately something can be done about the present situation, now, without procrastination and without changing anything in the Code of Canon Law. If the latter were indeed necessary we would be talking science-

[40] See R.G.W. Huysmans, "Bemerkingen bij de grondslag van een beroep tegen bestuurlijke handelingen in het recht van de Latijnse r.k. Kerk", in H. Warnink, ed., *Rechtsbescherming in de Kerk*, Leuven, 1991, 59.

fiction, and we have already said that this is not our intention.

Thus, the administrative courts of law foreseen for the future are missing from the Code of Canon Law. The motivation for the elimination *in extremis* of these planned agencies was never officially made public. One must assume that Church politics played a role as much as problems of legal theory.[41] The ecclesial-political motive lay in the vast differences in the world church which would make it difficult to impose a uniform regulation. Within the Church, this could have led to inequalities in the protection of rights, which did not seem desirable. The second motive was perhaps more important. The establishment of administrative courts would have brought with it that bishops, in certain cases, would be subject to the legal power of deacons and lay persons, among others, since now the latter can also be appointed judge. Many considered this to be a horror story which they would prefer not to experience personally.

The elimination of the administrative courts from the Code of Canon Law does not really take away the fact that a bishop possesses the competence to set up a true administrative court on the diocesan level all the same. It would have to ascertain whether the authorities are following the laws which they themselves promulgated, without ruling on whether the decision taken was opportune. In civil law this was already achieved some time ago. Within the Church I would consider this a remarkable achievement, a prophetic deed leading to an enormous increase in the credibility of the institutional

---

[41] K. Lüdicke, "Rechtsschutz gegenüber der Verwaltung in der Kirche: Experimente, Planungen, Perspektive", in H. Warnink, ed., *Rechtsbescherming in de Kerk*, Leuven, 1991, 43.

Church. However, I do not see the authorities immediately changing their position. Still, even less far-reaching legal procedures are possible.

In 1991 the Canon Law Society of America published a brochure entitled, "Protection of Rights of Persons in the Church."[42] In this text not only diocesan but even regional administrative courts were presented as a possibility. But two less formalized procedures, reconciliation and arbitration, are also legally well-delineated. The practical application of a number of these internal Church techniques for the protection of basic rights has led in several American dioceses to a reduction in the number of lawsuits in the civil courts. Numbers of Christians, both clergy and laity, would prefer a trustworthy internal church procedure. Only if this does not exist do they turn, sometimes reluctantly, to the civil courts.

In the Netherlands another model has already been made operational. Administrative courts or structural arbitration boards do not exist. However, on the level of the least juridical procedure, that is, organized reconciliation, some very fine work has already been done and shows a great deal of promise. In two dioceses, Utrecht and Breda, there is already a "Bureau for Disputes" whose goal is "to seek and to reach a fair solution, if a conflict has arisen between an ecclesial authority and a physical or legal person as a result of an administrative decree or the failure to carry out such an order." Thus, a Bureau for Disputes tries to prevent the escalation and the further juridicizing of a difference of opinion. Organized reconciliation functions as a partition between the conflict

---

[42] Canon Law Society of America, ed., *Protection of Rights of Persons in the Church: Revised Report of the Canon Law Society of America on the Subject of Due Process*, Washington, 1991.

which has arisen and the formal judicial process to be avoided if possible. Hopefully other dioceses will follow in the footsteps of Utrecht and Breda. As far as I know, there are similar projects underway in Haarlem, Groningen and Rotterdam. Expectations are running high for the long term. Not only can the bureaus make an important contribution to the prevention of the escalating number of disputes, the simple fact that they exist helps to create a mentality among both the authorities and those subject to them which will lead less easily to conflict.

In Belgium there is nothing. There was, however, a study by the Commission for Justice and Peace of Flemish Brabant with the intention of establishing a reconciliation commission. This study was inspired by the Bureau for Disputes of the diocese of Breda, but opted instead for a body with a broader responsibility. Even conflicts among lay persons among themselves could be brought before the reconciliation commission, according to the study. The fact that there was little hurry on the part of the Church authorities to implement the proposed, or another, procedure is lamentable. Well-equipped conciliatory bodies are of great importance to maintain the credibility of the Church. The brilliant message which it propagates threatens to lose its credibility whenever internal problems are not properly treated, or when the appropriate means of treatment exists but is insufficiently visible. Rights, human rights, stand or fall with the way in which they can be defended. The Church has nothing to lose with a properly organized and rightly applied mechanism for protection, but everything to gain. Let us remain sober and not use revelation as an argument to exchange reliable legal procedures for obscure (and not always free of domination) talk sessions, or the well-worn appeal to love. We can only agree with the canon lawyer, Robert Kennedy, when he says that revelation contains neither specific guidelines concerning the form of governmental activities in the Church, nor concerning structures connected with the protection of rights.[43]

The Long Road

Human rights in the Church need to be worked out in practice if they are to be more than a noncommittal declaration of principle. In order to function as the motor of a genuine culture of law within the Church, they must be formally superior to the remaining provisions in the Code of Canon Law. But even that in itself is not enough. The necessary procedures must be outlined in order to be able to enforce the protection of fundamental rights. In the long run, through the existence of reliable procedures, we can move automatically toward a clearer understanding of the content of the obligations and rights of all Christians. As a result of the concrete issues, colleges of law could begin thorough reflection on basic rights. It should be noted that examining an administrative decision for its compatibility with a fundamental right always requires a little bit of creative thinking by which the check on legality moves a step further than in the case of a purely technical law, due to the necessary vagueness of that basic right.

I understand that a certain skepticism could arise over this approach, a skepticism against a strategy which assigns a key position to the protection of rights in the

---

[43] R. Kennedy, "Commentary", in Canon Law Society of America, ed., *Protection of Rights*, 45-53.

struggle for human rights in the Church. I can hear people saying, can't we come up with anything more exciting? What about the case for women in ordained ministry? Isn't there a bigger dose of dynamite in confronting compulsory celibacy for priests with Article 12 of the European Treaty on Human Rights, which recognizes the right of man and woman to marry? Indeed, more attention for problems of this nature (which I experience as very real, harrowing and damaging for the credibility of the Church) heightens the show value of the issue being broached here.

The show value is even more dramatically heightened when we introduce these types of issues before the European Commission, and possibly before the European Court for Human Rights. For the moment, freedom of religion (Article 9), the victor in the struggle to balance the various rights and freedoms against each other, seems to be keeping them at bay.[44] Within the Church at present the latitude given to communities of faith can barely be restrained. But, of course, it is always a question of finding a balance.[45] One could imagine that the day will come when general social discrimination against women will be considered so abominable that the European Court will consider the canonical prohibition on the ordination of women to be in conflict with the European Convention on Human Rights. The argument which many use too easily, that the principle of the separation of church and state gives religions carte blanche to act however they

---

[44] J. Duffar, "La liberté religieuse dans les textes internationaux", *Revue du droit public et de la science politique en France et à l'étranger* 110 (1994) 939-967.
[45] D 7374/76, X. v. Denmark, 8 March 1976, DR 5/157; D 11045/84, Knudsen v. Norway, 8 March 1985, DR 42/268.

see fit within their own structures, simply does not work.

One example: neither in Belgium nor in the Netherlands can polygamous marriages be contracted. The principle of monogamy takes precedence over freedom of religion. Another example gives a more somber appearance but is not devoid of consequences. Some time ago the Court of Appeal in Mons (Belgium) ruled that the Catholic church is required to observe its own laws and, even more, that these laws must offer sufficient qualitative guarantees in the field of the protection of rights.[46] Subsequently, the Belgian Supreme Court, the *Cour de Cassation*, rejected the latter part of the decision but seemed to maintain the principle *patere legem quam ipse fecisti*, observe the law you issued yourself.[47] Both examples, that of polygamy which is more sensational and that of the more technical protection of rights, illustrate clearly that the freedom of internal organization and governance is not limitless for religions. The sky is not the limit. Legal procedures which still remain undecided in Strasbourg, will perhaps lead to other outcomes in the decades ahead. That cannot be predicted.

Nevertheless, I would not choose to go the way of the heavy content-related issues with numerous theological connotations, such as the position of women, the power of the Pope, celibacy, or democratic structures. I would even less opt for the hard confrontation in which a civil judge would have to cut through the knot. Although I

---

[46] Mons, 7 January 1993, *Revue de droit social* 80 (1993) 72, note R. Torfs.

[47] Cour de Cassation, 20 October 1994. See R. Torfs, "Le droit disciplinaire dans les églises", *Revue trimestrielle des droits de l'homme* 6 (1995) 245-270.

understand that many people, exhausted and disillusioned by so much senseless internal church rigidity, would choose this way, my preference remains — apart from a few moments of distracted powerlessness now and then — to continue on the path of gradual progress.

In this regard, the establishment of a proper protection of rights can fulfill a strategic role. Why? It is a method understandable and accessible to the hierarchy. It spares the church hierarchy the humiliation of being brought before the civil courts over internal conflicts with church members, conflicts which even in victory would leave scars. And problems which, often unjustly, are perceived by the hierarchy as very theologically loaded and over which they do not, or do not really, want to enter into discussion, can be placed between brackets for a while. The struggle for the protection of rights seems to be purely formal, but the existence and application of satisfactory legal procedures also has enormous content value in itself. The protection of rights is, with all its technicality and apparent neutrality, an excellent bridgehead to permit those who hold ecclesial responsibility to become slowly accustomed to a culture of law in the Church. This culture, partly because it is still an unknown, calls forth allergic reactions. But if this culture can gradually begin to seep into the system, if the *chain of law* regularly adds a new link or two, I am sure that the authorities will come to the conclusion after a time, that human rights in the Church are not a dangerous by-product of an egocentric Me-generation in a secular society, but are rather indispensable support pillars of an authentic and credible community of faith. Law can never replace faith, but it can insure that the unique message of Jesus is not obscured by Church structures which are no longer adapted to the sense of justice of the majority of Christians.

CHAPTER VI

FUNDAMENTAL RIGHTS AND
INDEPENDENT RESPONSIBILITY

An Approach that Takes the Initiative

In the previous chapter we examined the gradual growth of a culture of law. A few carefully selected subjects, such as the formal superiority of the obligations and rights of all the Christian faithful, can provide a workable starting point to make possible the theoretical and mental acceptance of basic rights among the Church hierarchy. The underlying assumption is that, in fact, a great deal is expected from these authorities. Their hesitation regarding fundamental rights does not change the fact that they are the ones who must make the final decisions. The formal superiority of Canons 208-223 is only present thanks to the hierarchy, who must have been convinced at some point that this superiority is necessary. The same goes for the protection of rights. Councils of reconciliation, colleges of arbitration, or administrative courts can be proposed by canon lawyers, theologians or committed church members, but if the authorities do not formally introduce them, all these conscientious workers for a better future for the Church wind up empty-handed. To summarize, the previous chapter presented how, partly under pressure from the grassroots, the authorities can be brought to consider basic rights as a mechanism leading to the development

of an open and welcoming governmental structure for the
Church.

If we link this train of thought with the theory of the
three approaches (macro-, meso- and micro-level) in the
second chapter which deals with a dynamic vision of law,
it is clear that up to now we have been looking at basic
rights from a potential meso-level, which translates into
the question of how a bishop can handle them in a creative manner. But, as we have already said in the second
chapter, basic rights also offer excellent possiblities for
action on the micro-level, possibilities for Christians to
exercise their own autonomous initiatives. Though inter-
ventions by the hierarchy might sometimes be called for,
these are often entirely unnecessary, whether in the form
of a formal intervention or via an approving nod of the
head. The perspective in every case is not that of the
church authorities, but that of the ordinary church member.

There is also a second reason, this time of a more tactical nature, to investigate more clearly whether Christians, by taking the initiative to fill in the content of
what is meant by basic rights, cannot assume more independent responsibility. Conservative church leaders
complain that many defenders of fundamental rights in
the Church are sullen, defensive figures, coldblooded
grouches who demand their rights, who lust after power
and status, and who suffer from a lack of humility and
service. An example of this line of thought occurred in a
speech at a congress of canon lawyers in Rome on 22
April 1993, given by the bishop of Fulda, Johannes
Dyba. Dyba said that, in regard to laity in the Church,
the discussion always seems to come back to leadership
(*Leiten*), not to achievement (*Leisten*), and that service

(*Dienen*) was apparently reserved to the priests.[48] Of course it is not for me to go into this specific quote from the bishop of Fulda, but rather the general atmosphere which it expresses. I think that we can promote a more dynamic approach, an approach derived from and supported legally by the obligations and rights of all the Christian faithful. We must get away from the tendency to employ fundamental rights as a means of securing particular rights, though this tendency is understandable in an institution, such as the church, which is, in the technical sense of the term, undemocratic. Seen from this perspective, fundamental rights serve as a dam against the discretionary power of the authorities, a power which is not always sufficiently restrained in practice.

However, basic rights are much more than an instrument for defense: to force them into this role betrays a nineteenth-century liberal mentality. Basic rights gain in moral authority, in the Church as well, whenever it is clear from their concrete coloration that they are not simply hollow demands made by the Me-generation but, on the contrary, that they raise the quality of life in the Church to a higher level.

I will attempt to work through this idea in two areas. First there is the discussion of the possible horizontal operation of fundamental rights. Thereafter the issue arises of how human rights can benefit the general welfare of the Church.

---

[48] J. Dyba, "Das hierarchische Weihepriestertum und das gemeinsame Priestertum aller Gläubigen: Kirchenrechtliche Überlegungen", in Pontificium Consilium de legum textibus interpretandis, ed., *Ius in vita et in missione ecclesiae*, Vatican City, 1994, 819.

The Horizontal Operation of Fundamental Rights

In civil law there is still some controversy on this point in many countries. Are fundamental rights valid only against the authorities, or must citizens take account of these basic rights in their relationships with each other as well? In the latter case, in the relationships of citizens with each other, it is a matter of what I would call the horizontal functioning of rights.

The controversy on this subject is still raging in civil law.[49] If one emphasizes the defensive and liberating aspect of fundamental rights, then their horizontal function is not really necessary. But a more modern view of basic rights as a constituent part of a social legal state offers many more possibilities.

I think that in this regard the Church has little reason to hesitate. We are confronted with yet another area in which canon law can serve as an example and a pioneer. That happened more often in the Middle Ages, but since then this tradition has been lost.

The horizontal operation of basic rights in the Church seems to me to be self-evident; they represent an ethical minimum which is not to be tampered with. In a community of faith in which, at least theoretically, violent conflicts of interest do not exist, the climate may never become clouded to such a degree that the functioning of fundamental rights among church members themselves becomes problematic. Basic rights are not only valid in opposition to a bishop, but a bishop himself enjoys basic rights in his capacity as a Christian. More progressive or more conservative church members are not allowed to

[49] K. Rimanque, ed., *De toepasselijkheid van grondrechten in private verhoudingen*, Antwerp, 1982.

treat each other as if Canons 208-223 do not exist. Even an annoying person has the right in the Church to a good reputation, which naturally does not imply that he or she cannot be subject to criticism. The presumption of good-will on the part of fellow Christians must always be present no matter what: if that does not occur on the basis of the Gospel, then it will at least be provided for via the horizontal operation of basic rights.

Whenever the horizontal operation is truly extended as far as, for example, the freedom of expression in Canon 212, par. 3, then one could conclude that the presence of a culture of dialogue in the Church is legally required. Dialogue means far more in this hypothesis than a formal conversation. Arriving at genuine dialogue seems to be a particularly difficult task. How do you transform the cold aloofness of a certain number of church leaders into a comfortable atmosphere in which a conversation can be at the same time pleasant and pertinent in content? Or is church politics by definition exclusively the art of subli-mating the impossible? Many people have been made deeply unhappy by constant, futile struggle with these issues, and often enough they have been driven to turn to means outside the Church in their search for meaning and happiness.

Fundamental Rights and the Common Good

Creatively grappling with basic rights via the notion of the common good seems even more dynamic than approaching the issue via the so-called horizontal func-tioning of rights, because it points more clearly to the per-sonal responsibility of church members. In Canon 223, par. 2 we read that, in the exercise of their rights, Christians must take into account the common good. In the past this passage has been seen too automatically as an instrument by which the authorities can intervene in a corrective way in case of irregularities.[50] But the same text can just as easily be taken to heart by the ordinary Christian. This means, among other things, that Christians are justified in making constructive and qualitatively strong suggestions regarding Church governance. Why not make an attempt, after thorough interdisciplinary study, to formulate a number of principles for reliable government and to present them to the Church authorities? And why not try to do this without rancor, without submissiveness, without postmodern cynicism? It is very difficult to continue to refuse pure quality.

Other suggestions can be made as well, such as a plea for the protection of rights or for a "woman-friendly" liturgy such as occurred in the 1991 Dutch report.[51]

Naturally a suggestion is only a suggestion. The authorities can read the proposals, can appreciate them or criticize them, and then carefully store them away in some forgotten file. While more open discussion takes place in the Netherlands, though not always in a way that radiates friendliness and politeness, in Flanders this technique of deliberate forgetfulness is applied with considerable zeal. I do not want to blow off steam over the official consultative body of the Flemish Church, the

---

[50] However, this interpretation is not correct. See R. Torfs, *Congregationele gezondheidsinstellingen. Toekomstige structuren naar profaan en kerkelijk recht*, Leuven, 1992, 150-151.

[51] *Een vrouwvriendelijke liturgie in de rooms-katholieke kerk. Advies van de werkgroep Vrouw en Kerk, de Katholieke Raad voor Kerk en Samenleving en de Unie Nederlandse Katholieke Vrouwenbewegingen aan de Nederlandse bisschoppen*, September 1991.

Interdiocesan Pastoral Council. Many people have thrown themselves into it with great commitment. But the results do not measure up to the quality and the number of proffered suggestions, certainly not when the issues involve relations and structures within the Church. Making recommendations which remain only recommendations cannot go on forever.

Moreover, the relationship between scholarly research and the Church authorities seems to be permeated by an atmosphere of suspicion. The position of the hierarchy seems to be reducible to the idea that research is research, and governance is governance. The respective territories are walled in and even surrounded by barbed wire. The view seems to be that if the church authorities respect the domain of academic research, then theologians ought to avoid activities which put the church's leadership under pressure. *Forcer la main* is not part of their mission statement.

This silent demarcation of the boundaries is not a happy development. First of all, I do not see why the independence of scholarly research needs to be coupled with its practical irrelevance. The symmetry of the construction gives a false impression of logic and reasonableness. Why? The best thing (well, the better thing) would be to think in terms of a gentleman's agreement by which freedom of research would be guaranteed, as prescribed in Canon 218 of the Code of Canon Law, and by which, at the same time, the results of the research would be taken very seriously, without the authorities surrendering their power to judge. Scholarship in theology is more than just a leisure occupation.

Scholarship is not free of obligations. To some degree it can be nonthreatening, although not completely, as for example when it focuses on clerical dress as it did in the

Middle Ages. But an ecclesiologist or a canon lawyer whose ideas are not the slightest bit confrontational to the authorities falls far short professionally, in spite of the encouraging slaps on the back that Church leaders might give out at formal receptions. In this way ecclesiologists and canon lawyers do not differ much, *mutatis mutandis*, from political scientists and constitutional lawyers in secular society.

There is a second reason why sharply differentiating the "territory" between church authorities and church scholars seems objectionable to me. If, on the one hand, one considers care for the common good to be a task for all Christian believers, and, on the other hand, one accepts the horizontal operation of basic rights, then disregarding scholarly research and refusing to enter into dialogue constitutes a violation of the law.

Parallel Circuits

An approach which takes the initiative concerning human rights using positively articulated basic rights relies more on the personal responsibility of Christians than an approach which simply claims rights defensively from the extant legal system. However, even constructive and cooperative reflection, based on one's own initiative, which takes the common good as its point of departure, often runs up against a wall of incomprehension in today's church with its somewhat rigid structures. For example, there are a small number of bishops with whom a conversation is either impossible or a hopeless fling at martyrdom, a remarkable fact in the light of the Good News. Remarkable, but unfortunately real. The question is what a Christian who finds the Church potentially too valuable to walk out on, is to do in such a situation. Is it not a viable choice in these circumstances to evade a direct confrontation with the legislators, not to set oneself directly against their power but to map out one's own path, far from all the power-games and their lamentable side-effects? At this point we are dealing with a completely different strategy, that of the parallel circuits and alternative ways of being Church. This approach not infrequently generates a rather adolescent thrill of triumph, a sense that one is finally standing on one's own feet.

Up to a certain point this sort of policy is entirely legitimate and based on the Code of Canon Law itself. A key provision is Canon 215 which guarantees freedom to form associations and hold meetings. This clause is new in the 1983 Code. It undoubtedly offers a range of possibilities.

How broad? Can we generate alternative financial sources in order to finance a number of activities which ultimately compete with the projects of the bishops? One can certainly go one's own way in this direction, but then not without some limitations.

Canon 222, par. 1 says that, "The Christian faithful are obliged to assist with the needs of the Church so that the Church has what is necessary for divine worship, for apostolic works and works of charity and for the decent sustenance of ministers." It nowhere says that this must occur via financing of the hierarchical authorities. The concept of "Church" is not developed further in this canon. It seems to me that, in any case, church members must contribute enough to provide for the decent sustenance of ministers, but that beyond that they

must be free in the fulfillment of their obligation to contribute.

There is another, more fundamental argument against
alternative financial means: "An office entailing the full
care of souls, for whose fulfillment the exercise of the
priestly order is required, cannot be validly conferred
upon someone who has not yet received priestly ordination" (Canon 150). This means that when competing
agencies are established the basic structure of the Church
hangs in the balance. I understand this argument, but
legally it is not easily clarified, certainly not when one
also tries to do adequate justice to the freedom of association with all its consequences. Although original initiatives together with their own means of financial support
are legal in themselves, a certain amount of caution is still
required. A perfectly legal competition with the hierarchical Church will turn out to be difficult to justify. Developing activities in areas which are not covered, or which
are neglected or abandoned by the official Church, seems
to me to be not only reconcilable with the Code, but is a
way of acting entirely in line with the freedom of association and the missionary task of the Christian believer
(Canon 211). In addition, it appears that if we take into
account the present criteria for ordination and Church
leadership as currently exercised, there will be more and
more arenas in which the institutional Church, in the
strict sense, can no longer take responsibility. Thus there
is fortunately a good deal of room for autonomous action
on the part of church members, in which a competitive
position over against the official Church structures is
absolutely not necessary.

A justification for autonomous activity on the part of
church members could also be inspired, and partly sup-

ported, by the sharing of competency in the right to form associations. Public associations, founded by the hierarchy, are exclusively authorized to teach Christian doctrine in the name of the Church or to promote public worship or to pursue other goals which by their nature are reserved to the same ecclesiastical authority (Canon 301, par.1). All other arenas are in principle covered by private associations which, in comparison with the Church authorities, enjoy a far greater degree of autonomy. But there is an exception: if the fulfillment of certain goals by private initiatives is insufficiently guaranteed — for example in the fields of education and care of the sick — then the Church authorities are competent to establish public associations here as well. We could summarize the foregoing with this principle: public associations have a reserved zone, private associations cover the rest of the territory. If the latter fall short, then public associations can fill the gap. Underlying this rule is the assumption that private initiatives are in danger of proving inadequate, but that the Church hierarchy always stands firm. It closes the breaches whenever private initiatives fail.

A question occurs to us at this point, a question which is highly charged. Should we, dare we, may we begin from the opposite starting point and employ an analogous argument regarding the day to day life and government of the church? The hierarchy is getting weaker, perhaps not in the certainty with which it governs, but in the fact that there is simply less to govern. In the Western world, where ordination is no longer a social promotion and the present criteria for ordination scare off many committed Christians, the personnel of the Church is diminishing. Instead of more priests per parish, there are more parishes

per priest. This alone will lead increasingly to the decline
of liturgy and the administration of sacraments. There are
gaps everywhere. Lay persons can, of course, engage in
parish work as volunteers but are they required to do so?
Could they also not involve themselves beyond tradi-
tional territorial parish structures and take over tasks
which until recently were taken care of by the parish?
And wouldn't these activities prove more satisfying,
because the tiring confrontation with Church structures
constantly demands mountains of energy?

Again, as long as there is no competition with official
structures, as long as only that space is filled which has
become free, and accordingly only those needs are met
which have been neglected, there is no danger. The personal responsibility of church members, as derived from a
positive reading of the notion of basic rights, offers a
good deal of legal support for this idea. Moreover, the
analogy with the right to form associations reveals how
the process of filling gaps, though perhaps on another
level and in a different direction, is mapped out concretely in the Code of Canon Law. If, indeed, the contin-
uation of the story of God is more important than legal
structures, then a policy such as the above can hardly be
contested.

Naturally there are other questions than the purely theoretical. If one wants to establish a parallel circuit which
is not competitive, then, of course, one needs money. In
the Netherlands, where the Church is responsible for its
own financial support and, in addition, a long and gener-
ous tradition of fund-raising exists, collecting a considerable amount of money does not seem to be impossible. In
Belgium the situation is different. The ministers of the
cult are paid by the state, whereby the Church is *de facto*

exempt from financial responsibility on a large scale. Gifts from church members are marked by their modesty. A dime in the collection basket. Perhaps that emphasizes more emphatically their symbolic character, but it bodes ill for whoever is responsible for the financial side of the establishment of a non-competitive parallel circuit.

Internal Emigration and Schism

In general I would not support overly forceful solutions when discussing alternative forms of church. Loosening one's connection with the Church, an attitude which does not formally reject the authority of the hierarchy but rather accepts it with cold suspicion or denies it with false naivety, does not appeal to me. We might call this "internal emigration." The Church members in question are no longer truly open to dialogue with the bishop. This seems to be a wrong-headed solution in any case, even (and especially) when the bishop involved seems himself to have consigned the word "dialogue" to a category of swear-words to be avoided. Together with "parallel circuits" or alternative forms of church, internal emigration produces all sorts of sociological leaders with no formal legitimacy who, for that reason alone, are slippery and uncontrollable, powered by the waves of their personal charisma. The desire for power is, after all, a dimension of our humanity.

I want to deal just briefly with the question of schism, a possibility which is raised now and then, in a strikingly facile manner, as a possible way to go. It seems to be the type of thing one ruminates over on a summer's evening after a few glasses of wine. The pleasure it brings is short-lived, however. Schism simply creates new popes as it were, men and women who, after their moment of glory, will suddenly begin to manifest less attractive traits.

Personal Responsibility and the Place of the Hierarchy

In this chapter we have considered taking the initiative in filling in the content of the obligations and rights of all Christians according to the Code of Canon Law, Canons 208-223.

To begin with, we looked for techniques which could serve to remove basic rights from an often criticized, negative atmosphere. A recognition of their horizontal function, and a cooperative endeavor to promote the common good within the Church via basic rights, both presented attractive starting points. But, at the same time, it appears that the climate of dialogue in which this approach can work to everyone's benefit, is missing now and then in the Church. Can one take further legal measures? Are "parallel circuits," possibly with their own financial resources, permissible? I believe that their existence, based among other things upon fundamental rights, can be justified on condition that they do not set out to compete with the Church authorities. Internal emigration and schism do not fulfill this criterion and therefore must be rejected.

A further question which can be raised in this regard is as follows: If basic rights are no longer applied to stimulate the authorities to take initiatives, but are used to build parallel circuits protected by law, then what is the place of ecclesial authority? Is it not being treated with veiled contempt, as in the case of internal emigration? Is there perhaps a hidden agenda hiding behind basic rights, namely, the wish to destroy ancient church structures which always accorded the bishop a central role?

This must not occur under any circumstances. The dialogue is not closed and the juridical leadership of the bishop is beyond discussion. If his actions fall within the jurisdictional limits of the Code, then this will be accepted. The bigger problem has to do with the possible sociological leadership of the bishop.

Bishops who, in our society, bear their undemocratic appointment to office and their much too unlimited responsibilities as a heavy burden, need to be strong to radiate some form of sociological leadership in addition to their legitimate formal powers. They are perceived less and less spontaneously by ordinary mortals (particularly among the younger generation) as shepherds of the people of God on a journey of faith, but more as leaders who are set against democratic structures as well as, for God knows what reason, against simple cheerfulness. In short, bishops today often find themselves saddled with an entire package of prejudices to be overcome. If a bishop succeeds in embodying some form of sociological leadership in spite of initial suspicion, then he deserves every praise. If he does not succeed, then the laity can manage to find sources of inspiration elsewhere without dethroning the bishop. In this approach he would remain bishop, but would be less and less a player in the most significant issues, issues of meaning and doubt, of life and death. The bishop must legally be recognized as such, he is and remains the shepherd of his diocese but, at the same time, it is not carved in stone that he must serve as the primary source of inspiration for everyone. Leadership is important, but it does not need to be determinative for the whole of life. When leadership is no longer overdrama-tized, the lives of the leaders themselves will brighten up considerably.

At the same time the laity, who have developed their own initiatives based on their fundamental rights, need to maintain a healthy measure of self-criticism. We must keep from overestimating ourselves, especially in a period in which the hierarchical Church, partly through its own fault, is experiencing a sharp decline. It is not because the hierarchy more obviously than ever does not seem to know everything, that the laity must suddenly step in. We may never give free rein to our righteous anger without at the same time taking some distance from our own reactions. Perhaps a number of our failures and frustrations are simply due to our own pettiness. But those who suggest that all of them are, should not be taken at their word.

I can imagine that not everyone will be satisfied with this explanation. A plea for noncompetitive parallel cir-cuits goes together with a reaffirmation of the legal posi-tion of the bishop as well as a warning against an overes-timation of themselves by the people at the grassroots. Isn't there some friction here? Undoubtedly. The unlim-ited authority of the pope (Canon 331) and the broad scope of power belonging to the bishop (Canon 381) sometimes collide with the obligations and rights of all the Christian faithful when these go a step beyond verbal formulation to the level of practical juridical application. At that point the principle of scarcity tempers the rhetoric. For basic rights set limits on the power of the authorities, and the power of the authorities limits the power of basic rights. The interpretation which one gives to the letter of the law depends ultimately on the starting point one chooses, that is, the macro-, meso- or micro-level presented in the second chapter. Depending on the starting point or the point of view, the law can be explained more to the advantage of one party or the other. But, on purely legal grounds, the model of powerful domination by the authorities is not per se superior to a structure in which basic rights are more expansive and the whole system takes on a more democratic hue, and vice versa. On a purely theological level they reflect the old dichotomies which even the Second Vatican Council could not overcome in a definitive synthesis.

CHAPTER VII

IN SEARCH OF HEALTHY RIVALRY

Lines of Force and Conclusions

The previous chapter forms the conclusion of the line
of reasoning which I have tried to elaborate in this book.

The starting point, in the first chapter, was the ambivalent attitude of the hierarchy of the Church toward human
rights in society. The hierarchy provided some encourage-
ment on the one hand, but on the other hand attempted to
block the spread of human rights in nineteenth-century
society. Now that this struggle has been engaged, questions arise concerning the position of human rights in the
Church. The ecclesial authorities are not exactly open
supporters of human rights, partly due to terminological
problems (regarding terms such as human rights and
democracy), and partly because of deeper motivations
such as the struggle with power, concern for orthodoxy,
and a rather unsubtle understanding of law.

We can however tinker a bit with this rather uninspired
approach to law. Law need not amount to a mechanical
monolith of standards. Chapter Two elaborates on this
idea, making it clear that law is not an unequivocal concept. There are a number of legal traditions. Canon law in
fact includes a very high number of open legal norms
which lend themselves to more than one interpretation in
an entirely legitimate manner. Because of these open laws

and because of the multiplicity of ecclesiological approaches which showed up in the conciliar documents during
the Second Vatican Council, the Code of Canon Law can
be read on at least three different levels. The reading on
the macro-level looks at law through the eyes of the
Pope; the meso-level is primarily that of the bishops; and
the ordinary Christian can construct an approach to law
on the micro-level using the obligations and rights of all
Christian believers. From all of this law emerges as a
flexible discipline. This methodological approach ought
to be applied to the existing laws in order to attain a
better understanding of basic rights in the Church.

What do these existing laws amount to? In the third
chapter we examined the history of how they evolved.
The theme of basic rights has been a major issue primarily since the Second Vatican Council. Juridical, theological and anthropological theories were formulated concerning the doctrine of law. For their part, legislators
considered for some time issuing a separate constitution
of the Church with a place for fundamental rights. This
project failed, and fundamental rights, which from then
on were more modestly termed the obligations and rights
of all Christian faithful, wound up in the 1983 Code, in
Canons 208-223. The composition of the present list of
basic rights does not show signs of any specific theological, juridical or anthropological approach. The legislators
seem to have worked eclectically. It is true however that
laws must be interpreted juridically as far as possible in
order that they mean something in practice.

But which "obligations and rights of all the Christian
faithful" are recognized concretely, here and now, in the
Code of Canon Law? Chapter Four began with a list and
then proceeded to focus on three fundamental rights.

From the analysis of these three, the principle of equality, the freedom of expression, and the freedom of theological research, we saw how widely varied the interpretations can be. Perhaps the legislator intended a fairly defensive formulation, but once the law was promulgated the genie was out of the bottle. The law leads a life of its own.

Chapter Five dealt with the question of how basic rights can be accepted in fact, now that they really are a part of canon law, accepted not only by the laity whose flexibility has been broadened, but also by the authorities who remain skeptical, as we said in the first chapter. My basic thought here is that fundamental rights will only have a chance of being accepted by everyone, and thus by the hierarchy, if a culture of law can be carefully built up. Two steps are necessary for its construction.

First, one would have to develop in a more focused way the idea that the obligations and rights of all the Christian faithful hold formal preeminence over other norms in canon law, and therefore enjoy priority in case of legal conflict. Secondly, one would have to work on securing appropriate protection of these rights, seemingly a technical issue but with very deep connotations for content nonetheless. I would prefer this more gradual approach to a determinedly aggressive one, which might include calling upon the civil courts. The hierarchy needs to be brought to the acceptance of basic rights by means of dialogue.

But basic rights are not the exclusive property of an enlightened hierarchy seeking liveable church structures. Chapter Six illustrated how they can be directly appropriated by the laity. Even from their standpoint, the micro-level mentioned in the first chapter, the story of basic rights can be told. In this connection I made a plea for taking the initiative. Those who struggle for human rights can not only claim their rights, but also cooperate in developing an essentially valuable vision of human rights. An important role in this vision is played by the horizontal functioning of these rights, and by action and proposals brought forth by the laity, even on their own initiative, for the sake of the common good. If this proposal is going to have a chance of succeeding, then a dialogical attitude is demanded on the part of the authorities, and the strict division between administration and scholarship must be given up. If this dialogue is absent or unfruitful, the laity can go further in taking up their own initiatives. They can establish "parallel circuits," as long as these do not compete with the hierarchy and its institutions. In the many arenas in which the official Church can no longer assume responsibility due to lack of personnel (intellectual study, charity, faith and civil society for example), developing a separate internal structure is not only to be tolerated, but to be recommended. At the same time excesses such as internal emigration and schisms should be avoided. The recognition of the specific duties of the Church authorities should not be threatened, although they cannot always function as a source of inspiration and motivation in themselves.

So far this is my story on human rights in the Church, with particular attention to the micro-level, the standpoint of the laity, to "suburban canon law", as one could call this approach.

The Context of the Present Argument

From the beginning I have opted for a realistic point of departure. I said in the first chapter that I would not want to choose between history and science fiction. On the contrary, the point of departure is the here and now, the Church as it is today, with the system of law as it is conceived at the present moment, including all the gray areas which characterize it. The path we have followed is that of a gradual reform, based on dialogue, with law as an elastic enclosure.

The approach is fairly pragmatic, although I think it is not free of illusions. In political terms it is rather centrist. But I have tried to avoid the extreme center, because those who try anxiously to situate themselves in that center have no identity of their own. They tend to float and drift on the waves of fashion and public opinion. If there is a pull to the right the extreme centrist will follow reluctantly. If leftist ideas suddenly gain a following the extreme centrist will make eyes at the left, searching for the midpoint among the midpoints. The extreme centrist arouses extremist ideas amongst his or her right or left-wing opponents, who primarily seek refuge away from a colorless lack of horizon.

I can imagine that the path we have followed in this book might hold little appeal for youth. Although that is not necessarily a disaster for a product which was not aimed at the youth market, this fact should make us stop and think. The specter of a dead-end street is looming. Nobody wants to be the last one out the door. Indeed those who are not already themselves totally devoted to the Church (perhaps in view of an almost Proustian longing for things past) would not be stimulated to take an interest in the Church by the very tactical argument which has been developed here. For that reason I want to relativize clearly the argument presented here. It is not intended to be an inexhaustible spiritual spring. It is not a compendium for spirituality, nor a profession of faith. It is intended to be employed alongside those indispensable aids to greater spiritual depth in the cause of a liveable, welcoming and hospitable church, a church that knows neither anxiety nor bitterness.

But is this approach the right one for our times? Should we not commit our cause to the Holy Spirit and leave tactics to politicians and football coaches? Or, to put the case very differently, why bother so much about a system which doesn't work any more? Isn't caution an excuse for cowardice? In short, why not take the radical road, why tread the middle path? This question cannot be avoided.

Why not Less Action and More Trust?

"The Spirit of Pentecost has abandoned many churches and institutes because there are too many arguments and often uncharitable discussions about one's own 'right-ness' and the other's complete 'wrongness.' God who is Love can only be active where there is love."[52]

A simple quotation, but it serves to illustrate a charis-matically-inspired call to exchange discussion (some-times called argument — the two concepts run closely parallel to each other) for the Holy Spirit. It would never be expressed so bluntly, but covertly the starting point is not infrequently the presupposition of a dichotomy between the two approaches. It is *either* discussion *or* the Holy Spirit. Is it not preferable to opt for the latter, since it seems more secure? Discussion runs the risk that the

[52] See *Een-twee-een*, 11 June 1993, 5.

positions will harden, often leading directly to conflict. Shouldn't calm acceptance take the place of action, the acceptance of, and surrender to, that which fascinates, such as finds place in faith?

There is much to be said for calm acceptance, even independently of charismatic and philosophical considerations. Some canon lawyers take their inspiration from the seasoned tiller of the soil who has learned to patiently let nature take her course. After all, time heals all wounds. Older, less democratically inclined Church leaders cannot resist the laws of human biology. They, too, will pass. They will be replaced by a younger generation who know the meaning of cooperation, dialogue and personal responsibility. Human rights, too, are part of the inheritance this younger generation brings with it. That, at least, is the view of some.

I am afraid that those who wait are wrong. First, I do not believe in waiting, but in watching. Secondly, the belief in a new generation which is liberated from the confines of authoritarian thought testifies to naive optimism. Even in secular society, 1968 has produced more materialistic advertising executives than noble-minded practitioners of love of neighbor. Today, paradoxically, one hears the statement that more often than not it is the older church leaders who seem most sympathetic to independence and human rights.

Many idealistic young people do not opt anymore for forms of action in the Church. They choose instead for involvement outside the Church, although "outside the Church" is in fact the wrong term. They do not see the Church as an appropriate forum for the expression of their commitment. They want to be engaged in the nitty gritty of service to the world. Naturally there are still a handful (or more, let's not be miserly) of socially-inspired idealists in supply within the Church. But not too many. The Church today attracts another type of person. There are a number of young intellectuals active in the Church for whom human rights or democratic structures are anything but a concern. Apart from a small number of fundamentalists who have no future in any case, I am thinking of two categories.

First there are those whom I would call, perhaps a bit sloppily, new pietists. In an interview with *Herder Korrespondenz*, Gérard Defois, then archbishop of Sens and Auxerre in France, said that youth within the Church are more attracted by spirituality groups and movements.[53] They accuse their elders — those over 40 — of being more occupied with sociology than theology and they plead for a new spirituality. Human rights hold little or no interest for such people. They choose the way of the Holy Spirit over any discussion.

In addition there is another group with which, unlike the previous one, I have difficulty: the young intellectuals who need a quiet and well-anchored faith in their life. Members of this group keep themselves just as occupied with their social and financial development as with the needs of their families. They commit their spiritual life to the Church, but they expect it to hand them ready-made answers. Life always presents so many worries. Again, for older persons such an attitude seems a little more appropriate since they have a right to rest, but it raises questions for young people. The appearance of obedience really points to a disinterest in content.

In short, waiting leads to nothing. It is an attitude . which not infrequently goes together with diminished

---

[53] See "Das Gesicht des französischen Katholizismus ändert sich", *Herder Korrespondenz*, March 1992, 128-133.

perception and a constriction of consciousness. It is a method of approach which can hardly be reconciled with an idea which is very precious to me, the mysticism of the open eyes, as described by Johann Baptist Metz. By means of this idea Metz interprets the parable of the Good Samaritan. The priest passes by and sees nothing. The Levite passes by and sees nothing. And then comes the Samaritan, a somewhat inferior figure. And he sees. To be Christian means to see more than others do.[54]

To see and to act — action is clearly involved according to Metz — have little place where waiting enjoys priority. Attention and observation which precede astonishment must be present in a Christianity which hopes to be attractive. In any case, whether what is at stake is art or science or love or faith, the ability to pay close attention and to observe clearly are indispensable to quality. As the Central European poet Paul Celan wrote, attention is the mystical prayer of the soul.

The false dilemma between the work of the Holy Spirit and the initiatives belonging to the laity must be unmasked. And time brings absolutely no wisdom. Why can't surrender to faith be coupled with the mysticism of the open eyes and effective action within the church structures where everything is in danger of going wrong? Whoever only waits, falls short.

Why not More Action and Less Trust?

A reform-colored approach which takes the existing legal order as its point of departure might seem too weak

---

[54] See *Welches Christentum hat Zukunft? Dorothee Sölle und Johann Baptist Metz im Gespräch met Karl-Josef Kuschel*, Stuttgart, 1990, 29.

to a number of conscious and active laity. After many
years of talking to a brick wall in the Church is it still
possible to make a case for dialogue within the existing
structures? Are we fooling ourselves?

This is not a question that can be brushed aside. Of
course, if you are a supporter of the gradual way you can
justify your choice by pointing to the possible positive
results in the long term — the eschatology of the
reformer. But at the same time those who keep the law in
mind can never be certain that they are innocent. In his
fascinating book, *Face à l'extrême*, the French-Bulgarian
author Tzvetan Todorov, writing about the crimes of the
Hitler regime, says something unforgettable: "La leçon
des crimes nazis est que ceux qui appliquent la loi sont
plus dangereux que ceux qui l'enfreignent." (The lesson
of the Nazi crimes is that those who apply the law are
more dangerous than those who break it.)[55]

Certainly all of this needs to be set in an appropriate
context — the Church is not a concentration camp. But
doesn't there exist in the Church something like collaboration with the enemy? I'm not referring to the very
unsubtle collusion of the executioner, but the less dis-
cernible collaboration of the intellectual. Wouldn't such
persons understand better than anyone else the art of
describing their lack of moral courage as tactical mastery
in such a way that they begin to believe it themselves?
The question is difficult to answer simply. Not every
form of nuancing amounts to cowardice, and a sense of
tactics is not necessarily a lack of courage. But we must
dare to put the choices we make in a broader context.
Why do we speak the way we speak? What sort of hidden

---

[55] T. Todorov, *Face à l'extrême*, Paris, 1991, 138 in a passage where
the author cites Dwight MacDonald.

motive might co-determine the position we take? Here, too, the mysticism of open eyes is important.

Some time ago, during the pause at a lecture in the Netherlands, I received a written question: "Do you really think that weaving through the text of the law in the way that you propose, with all its bypassing and dodging, can be reconciled with the attitude of Jesus?" This is a pertinent question. Radicalism might give way to a Pharisaical approach, in the name of Jesus. A reform-minded approach loaded down with tactical consider- ations is certainly unacceptable when it stands alone. Church politics should not be reduced to *Realpolitik*. A reformist approach must be combined with two other ele- ments if it is to be credible, and those are clarity and suf- ficient attention to utopias.

By clarity I do not mean one-dimensional simplemind- edness, but in fact the absence of a split between what one says and what one really thinks. Caution in formulat- ing these ideas should not disguise their essence. One needs to have the courage, for example, to affirm clearly the untenable nature of compulsory celibacy for the clergy and the prohibition of the ordination of women, in such a way that this would not again lead to violent explosions against church leaders. On the other hand, it is not necessary that one say calmly of every explosive issue in the church that it needs a great deal of further study. A friendly clarity must be possible.

Besides clarity we should not lose sight of the need for utopias. In the first chapter of this book I said I did not want to deal with science-fiction. By that I meant that it makes little sense to take an image of a possible future as if it apparently does exist or can exist, and use it as a point of departure for action here and now. Fostering a vision of utopia is something different, It means dreaming of ideal, or in any case of better, church structures. In the Church, as in secular society, our most important mission today is building castles in the sky.[56] Utopia is indispensable in the search for goals and institutions to strive for.

But even when clarity is promoted and utopias are not shot down in a burst of soulless realism, it can happen that conscious and enthusiastic Christians do not wish to travel the path of steady reform — perhaps out of impatience, perhaps also because they want to live in truth here and now, because a life without authenticity seems worthless to them. Perhaps also because they are not simple people. And sometimes undoubtedly also because they long for genuineness and, at the same time, are not always equally flexible.

These radical Christians, even within the existing structures, have the right to be more radical than they themselves generally suspect. Two techniques are particularly striking in this regard, namely the fomation of habits or customs which, under certain circumstances, can even contradict the law,[57] and the non-reception of a law which can be invoked in limited cases.[58]

---

[56] See U. Bermbach, *Demokratietheorie und politische Institutionen*, Opladen, 1991, 258. The author cites the American social scientist Lewis Mumford.

[57] R.G.W. Huysmans, *De normis generalibus. Algemene normen van het kerkelijk recht. Boek I van het r.k. wetboek van canoniek recht*, Leuven, 1993, 128.

[58] K. Walf, *Vragen rondom het nieuwe kerkelijk recht*, Hilversum, 1988, 44. The *ius remonstrandi* is a specific form of non-reception. See for example P.G. Caron, "'Ius remonstrandi' ed appello per abuso nella dottrina dei canonisti", in *Studi in onore di P.A. D'Avack*, Milan, 1976, I, 539-590; E. Labandeira, "La 'remonstratio' y la aplicación de las leyes universales en la iglesia particular", *Ius Canonicum* 24 (1984) 711-740.

But what if they go even further? Purely in terms of canon law this would constitute illegality. Of course, that does not mean that they stop being a Christian believer, or that they do not belong to the Church anymore.

Extreme caution is advised in regard to illegality. Although it does not seem to me the way to go, I would not want to write it off as necessarily negative and sinful. In the same way, civil disobedience in secular society is in a large number of cases absolutely not threatening to the system. Usually one single law is broken while the entire body is accepted, and even more: sometimes the violation of a law occurs out of respect for society as a whole. Civil disobedience against laws which discriminated on the basis of skin color in the United Sates were not intended to subvert or overthrow the state, but instead to qualitatively improve the legal system which, as such, was not called into question. The intention of civil disobedience was to achieve justice by means of a violation of the law.

In the Biblical tradition the concept of justice is of central importance. Let me offer one example. A commentary on the daily prayer of Jews, the Eighteen-Prayer, proposes in regard to law and justice: "Law must not be such that it ruins people. Yes, the danger that people will come to ruin must even be eliminated before one can speak of law... Law and justice are not synonyms, but they are also not opposites; law only becomes reality when justice is embodied in it"[59].

[59] On this point see P. Stevens, "Ecclesia sancta simul et purificanda. Op zoek naar verdere rechtsbescherming van de gelovige in de Kerk", in H. Warnink, ed., *Rechtsbescherming in de Kerk*, Leuven, Peeters, 1991, 141-154. P. Stevens takes the quotation from D.J. van der Sluis, et al., "Elke Morgen Nieuw. Inleiding tot de Joodse gedachtenwereld

Whenever the struggle for justice, however imperfectly it might be expressed, collides with positive law, we should think very carefully before throwing the first stone.

In Search of Healthy Rivalry

Ultimately neither the patient tiller of the soil nor the passionate revolutionary can be the enemy of those who strive toward a reform of church structures based on human rights, and who wish to accomplish it gradually. Even the church authorities, inspired by the same unsurpassed message of Jesus, are not the enemy in these often dismal times, a characteristic shared in common with other times. More than ever, Christians must not close ranks (closed ranks have little charm). Rather, they must seek to promote healthy rivalry. They must enter into dialogue with each other, conscious of the relativity of their own standpoints and of their differences of opinion, and conscious as well of the power of the message which they try to embody, each in his or her own manner. In a time in which tax specialists are important and lawyers remain important, in which "cool" is better than "clean," fast is better than beautiful and sly is better than clever, many expect from their faith and the Church a liveable environment and less gratuitous affirmation. According to Jürgen Habermas, truth loses its character, it exhausts its own definition, whenever it does not also reflect at the same time honesty and justice. And these

aan de hand van een van de centrale Joodse gebeden", in Y. Aschkenasy et al., *Handboek voor de studie van de Rabbijnse literatuur*, Hilversum, 1978, 254-255.

characteristics lack all content if there is no discussion and dialogue.

I am not talking about battle scenarios in which those who have right on their side express their rightness in hostile torrents of abuse. I am speaking instead of a real conversation, lifted above the tragedy of tactical maneuvers, where one can be simply vulnerable. I refuse to believe that this does not square with faith. We must continue to oppose the clear-cut hardness of "no-nonsense" faith, precisely because faster is not more beautiful than beautiful. Discussion is slow and sometimes raises doubts, but it offers a habitable environment. I cannot conceive of a faith which is not habitable.

The enemy is not the fellow believer with different accents. The enemy is something else. The enemy lives inattentively and rigidly, avoids genuine doubt, depth and self-criticism. The enemy must be loved in any case, but is not for that reason to be less opposed.

The enemy is not the fellow believer with a somewhat different vision. This fellow believer must be treated within the church in such a way that Christian involvement and *joie de vivre* are not mutually incompatible concepts, and if that is not possible, that the paradox remains at least bearable. Within the Church structures as they now exist, with today's legal framework, this is possible to a very great extent due to the obligations and rights of all Christian believers. Human rights in the Church can, here and now, lead toward more democratic and more comfortable Church structures without necessarily changing the law. It was the goal of this book to focus attention on this point and to sketch out ways to make it all possible.

Naturally this does not conclude the story. *In via veritas*. As a canon lawyer my utopia consists of a legal structure within the Church which reflects a superior form of harmony — a harmony that has nothing to do with empty bliss and the absence of conflict, but is much closer to what the poet Maria Vasalis called, delightfully and enticingly, "an order in which chaos has its place."

SELECT BIBLIOGRAPHY

This list is by no means complete, and presents only a few suggestions for further reading.

AUBERT, R., "Religious Liberty from Mirari Vos to the Syllabus", *Concilium* 1:7 (1965) 89-105.

AYMANS, W., "Kirchliche Grundrechte und Menschenrechte", *Archiv für katholisches Kirchenrecht* 149 (1980) 389-409.

BEAL, J.P., "Protecting the Rights of Lay Catholics", *The Jurist* 47 (1987) 129-164.

BEAL, J.P., "Canon Law and the Rights of the Faithful", *New Theology Review* 7:3 (1994) 6-22.

BERMBACH, U., *Demokratietheorie und politische Institutionen*, Opladen, 1991.

BORGMAN, E., VAN DIJK, B. and SALEMINK, TH., eds., *Recht en onrecht in de rooms-katholieke kerk*, Amersfoort/Leuven, 1989.

Canon Law Society of America, ed., *Protection of Rights of Persons in the Church: Revised Report of the Canon Law Society of America on the Subject of Due Process*, Washington, 1991.

CARON, P.G., "'Ius remonstrandi' ed appello per abuso nella dottrina dei canonisti", in *Studi in onore di P.A. D'Avack*, Milan, 1976, I, 539-590.

CASTILLO LARA, R., "Some General Reflections on the Rights and Duties of the Christian Faithful", *Studia Canonica* 20 (1986) 7-32.

CENALMOR, D., *La Ley fundamental de la Iglesia: historia y análisis de un proyecto legislativo*, Pamplona, 1991.

CORECCO, E., "Erwägungen zum Problem der Grundrechte des Christen in Kirche und Gesellschaft: Methodologische Aspekte", *Archiv für katholisches Kirchenrecht* 150 (1981) 412-453.

CORECCO, E., HERZOG, N. and SCOLA, A., eds., *Die Grundrechte des Christen in Kirche und Gesellschaft*, Fribourg/Freiburg im Breisgau/Milan, 1981.

CORIDEN, J.A., "Human Rights in the Church: A Matter of Credibility and Authenticity", *Concilium* 124 (1979) 67-76.

CORIDEN, J.A. and ÖRSY, L., *The Case of Freedom: Human Rights in the Church*, Washington, 1969.

DANEELS, F., "The Right of Defence", *Studia Canonica* 27 (1993) 77-95.

DEL PORTILLO, A., "Ius associationis et associationes fidelium iuxta Concilii Vaticani II doctrinam", *Ius Canonicum* 29 (1989) 5-28.

DIET, M., "Die Gleichheit aller Glaübigen in der Kirche. Zu Kanon 208 des CIC 1983", *Theologie der Gegenwart* 31 (1988) 113-121.

DOE, N., "Canonical Doctrines of Judicial Pecedent: A Comparative Study", *The Jurist* 54 (1994) 205-215.

"Dossier: l'Affaire Gaillot", *Revue de droit canonique* 45 (1995) 75-162.

DREWERMANN, E., GREINACHER, N. and SÖLLE, D., *Wege der Befreiung sehen*, Ilsede, 1992.

DUFFAR, J., "La liberté religieuse dans les textes internationaux", *Revue du droit public et de la science politique en France et à l'étranger* 110 (1994) 939-967.

DYBA, J., "Das hierarchische Weihepriestertum und das gemeinsame Priestertum aller Gläubigen: Kirchenrechtliche Überlegungen", in Pontificium Consilium de legum textibus interpretandis, ed., *Ius in vita et in missione ecclesiae*, Vatican City, 1994, 807-821.

ERRAZURIZ, C.J., "Esiste un dirito di libertà religiosa del fedele all'interno della Chiesa?", *Fidelium iura* 3 (1993) 79-99.

ETCHEGARAY, R., "Culture chrétienne et droits de l'homme: du rejet à l'engagement", in Fédération Internationale des Universités Catholiques, ed., *Culture chrétienne et droits de l'homme*, Brussels/Louvain-la-Neuve, 1991, 3-15.

Fidelium iura, Journal of the University of Navarra in Pamplona, published beginning in 1991.

GREINACHER, N. and JENS, I., eds., *Freiheitsrechte für Christen? Warum die Kirche ein Grundgesetz braucht,* Munich, 1980.

HEIMERL, H., "Menschenrechte, Christenrechte und ihr Schutz in der Kirche", *Theologisch-praktische Quartalschrift* 121 (1973) 26-35.

HEIMERL, H., "Menschenrechte und Christenrechte", *Theologisch-praktische Quartalschrift* 139 (1991) 20-29.

HEINEMANN, H., "Menschenrechte? Eine Anfrage an das Kirchenrecht", *Archiv für katholisches Kirchenrecht* 143 (1974) 238-267.

HILPERT, K., *Die Menschenrechte: Geschichte, Theologie, Aktualität*, Dusseldorf, 1991.

HINDER, P., *Grundrechte in der Kirche. Eine Untersuchung zur Begründung der Grundrechte in der Kirche*, Fribourg, 1977.

HOLLAND, S., "Equality, Dignity and Rights of the Laity", *The Jurist* 47 (1987) 103-128.

HUYSMANS, R.G.W., *Het recht van de leek in de rooms-katholieke kerk van Nederland*, Hilversum, 1986.

KRÄMER, P., "Menschenrechte-Christenrechte: Das neue Kirchenrecht auf dem Prüfstand", in GABRIELS, A. and REINHARDT, H.F., eds., *Ministerium Iustitiae: Festschrift für Heribert Heinemann zum 60. Geburtstag*, Essen, 1985, 169-177.

KREMSMAIR, J., "Grundrechte im Codex Iuris Canonici 1983", *Österreichisches Archiv für Kirchenrecht* 42 (1993) 46-66.

LABANDEIRA, L., "La 'remonstratio' y la aplicación de las leyes universales en la iglesia particular", *Ius Canonicum* 24 (1984) 711-740.

LE TOURNEAU, D., "Quelle protection pour les droits et les devoirs fondamentaux des fidèles dans l'Eglise?", *Studia Canonica* 28 (1994) 59-83.

LO CASTRO, G., *Il soggetto e i suoi diritti nell'ordinamento canonico*, Milan, 1985.

LOCHMANN, J.H., "Les Églises réformées et la théologie des 'droits de l'homme'", *Revue Théologique de Louvain* 10 (1979) 348-352.

LOMBARDIA, P., "The Fundamental Rights of the Faithful", *Concilium* 5:8 (1969) 42-46.

LUF, G., "Grundrechte und kirchlicher Rechtsschutz. Erwägungen zu einer hermeneutischen Rechtstheologie", *Österreichisches Archiv für Kirchenrecht* 25 (1975) 25-54.

LUF, G., "Grundrechte im CIC/1983", *Österreichisches Archiv für Kirchenrecht* 35 (1985) 107-131.

NAVARRO, L., "Il principio costituzionale di uguaglianza nell'ordinamento canonico", *Fidelium iura* 2 (1992) 145-163.

NEUMANN, J., *Menschenrechte auch in der Kirche?*, Zurich/Cologne/Einsiedeln, 1976.

PILTERS, M. and WALF, K., eds., *Menschenrechte in der Kirche*, Dusseldorf, 1980.

PREE, H., "Die Meinungsaußerungsfreiheit als Grundrecht des Christen", in *Recht als Heilsdienst: Festschrift für M. Kaiser zum 65. Geburtstag*, Paderborn, 1989, 42-85.

PRIETO, A., "Los derechos subjetivos públicos en la Iglesia", *Revista Española de Derecho Canónico* 19 (1964) 856-891.

PROVOST, J., "Freedom of Conscience and Religion: Human Rights in the Church", in Fédération Internationale des Universités Catholiques, ed., *Culture chrétienne et droits de l'homme*, Brussels/Louvain-la-Neuve, 1991, 50-53.

PROVOST, J.H., "The Nature of Rights in the Church", in *Proceedings of the Canon Law Society of America*, 1991, 1-18.

PROVOST, J.H. and WALF, K., eds., *Ius sequitur vitam: Studies in Canon Law Presented to P.J.M. Huizing*, Leuven, 1991.

SCHNIZER, H., "Überlegungen zum normativen Gehalt von c. 212 CIC", in AYMANS, W. and GERINGER, K.-Th., eds., *Iuri Canonici Promovendi: Festschrift für Heribert Schmitz zum 65. Geburtstag*, Regensburg, 1994, 75-95.

SCHNUR, R., *Zur Geschichte der Erklärung der Menschenrechte*, Munich, 1974.

SCHWARTLANDER, J., ed., *Menschenrechte: Eine Herausforderung der Kirche*, Munich/Mainz, 1979.

SOLER, C., "El derecho fundamental a la palabra y los contenidos de la predicación", *Fidelium iura* 2 (1992) 305-331.

SWIDLER, L., *After the Absolute: The Dialogical Future of Religious Reflection*, Minneapolis, 1990.

TORFS, R., *De vrouw en het kerkelijk ambt. Analyse in functie van de mensenrechten in kerk en staat*, Leuven/Amersfoort, 1985.

TORFS, R., "Mensenrechten", in TORFS, R., ed., *Het nieuwe kerkelijk recht. Analyse van de Codex Iuris Canonici 1983*, Leuven, 1985, 130-167.

TORFS, R., "Estructura ecclesiástica y responsabilidad independiente: Reflexiones en torno a los cánones 212 §3 y 218 del CIC 1983", *Revista Española de Derecho Canónico* 47 (1990) 663-694.

TORFS, R., *Congregationele gezondheidsinstellingen. Toekomstige structuren naar profaan en kerkelijk recht*, Leuven, 1992.

TORFS, R., "Kerkstructuren, mensenrechten en gezelligheid", *Vlaanderen Morgen*, May-June 14 (1993) 9-19.

TORFS, R., *Mensen en rechten in de Kerk*, Leuven, 1993.

TORFS, R., "*Propria verborum significatio*: de l'épistémologie à l'herméneutique", *Studia Canonica* 29 (1995) 179-192.

VANDER STICHELE, C., VAN DER HELM, A., VAN DIJK, B., TORFS, R. and VELIŠČEK, S., eds., *Disciples and Discipline: European Debate on Human Rights in the Roman Catholic Church*, Leuven, 1993.

VILADRICH, P., *Teoría de los derechos fundamentales del fiel. Presupuestos críticos*, Pamplona, 1969.

WALF, K., "Die Menschenrechte in der katholischen Kirche", *Diakonia* 5 (1974) 376-388.

WALF, K., *Vragen rondom het nieuwe kerkelijk recht*, Hilversum, 1988.

WARNINK, H., TORFS, R. and DE ROO, P., eds., *De leek in de Kerk: mogelijkheden, grenzen en perspectieven*, Leuven, 1989.

WARNINK, H., ed., *Rechtsbescherming in de Kerk*, Leuven, 1991.

WARNINK, H., ed., *Ius propter homines*, Leuven, 1993.

Welches Christentum hat Zukunft? Dorothee Sölle und Johann Baptist Metz im Gespräch met Karl-Josef Kuschel, Stuttgart, 1990.

WORGUL, G.S., ed., *Issues in Academic Freedom*, Pittsburgh, 1992.